Textile

EDITED BY
CATHERINE HARPER
AND DORAN ROSS

THE JOURNAL OF
CLOTH AND CULTURE

VOLUME 4
ISSUE 1
SPRING 2006

ORDERING INFORMATION
Three Issues per volume. One volume per annum. 2006:
Volume 4

ONLINE
www.bergpublishers.com

BY MAIL
Berg Publishers
C/O Turpin Distribution Services
Pegasus Drive
Stratton Business Park
Biggleswade
Bedfordshire SG18 8TQ
UK

BY FAX
+ 44 (0)1767 601640

BY TELEPHONE
+ 44 (0)1767 604951

For Subscription Enquiries
email custserv@turpin-distribution.com

ENQUIRIES
Editorial: Kathryn Earle, Managing Editor,
email kearle@bergpublishers.com

Production: Ken Bruce,
email kbruce@bergpublishers.com

Advertising: Veruschka Selbach,
email vselbach@bergpublishers.com

SUBSCRIPTION DETAILS
Free Online Subscription for Print Subscribers.

Full color images available online.

Access your electronic subscription through
www.ingentaconnect.com

Institutional base list subscription price:
US$225.00, £125.00

Individuals' subscription price: US$79.00, £46.00

Berg Publishers is the imprint of
Oxford International Publishers Ltd.

AIMS AND SCOPE

Cloth accesses an astonishingly broad range of human experiences. The raw material from which things are made, it has various associations: sensual, somatic, decorative, functional and ritual. Yet although textiles are part of our everyday lives, their very familiarity and accessibility belie a complex set of histories, and invite a range of speculations about their personal, social and cultural meanings. This ability to move within and reference multiple sites gives textiles their potency.

This journal brings together research in textiles in an innovative and distinctive academic forum for all those who share a multifaceted view of textiles within an expanded feld. Representing a dynamic and wide-ranging set of critical practices, it provides a platform for points of departure between art and craft; gender and identity; cloth, body and architecture; labor and technology; techno-design and practice—all situated within the broader contexts of material and visual culture.

Textile invites submissions informed by technology and visual media, history and cultural theory; anthropology; philosophy; political economy and psychoanalysis. It draws on a range of artistic practices, studio and digital work, manufacture and object production.

SUBMISSIONS

Should you have a topic you would like us to consider, please send an abstract of 300–500 words to one of the editors. Notes for Contributors can be found at the back of the journal and style guidelines are available by emailing kbruce@bergpublishers.com or from the Berg website (www.bergpublishers.com).

ISSN: 1475-9756
www.bergpublishers.com

Contents

EDITORS

Catherine Harper
University College for the
Creative Arts at Epsom
Ashley Road
Epsom KT18 5BE
UK
charper@ucreative.ac.uk

Doran Ross
UCLA
Fowler Museum of Cultural History
308 Charles Young Drive
Los Angeles, CA 90095-1549
USA
dross@arts.ucla.edu

TEXTILE FORUM is a quarterly magazine for people interested in the following fields of textiles:

- Arts, crafts and industry
- Cultural heritage
- Education

TEXTILE FORUM offers, above all, a platform for discussions and aims to promote cross-cultural and interregional dialogue. The magazine would like to build bridges between people in the various fields of textiles.

The European Textile Network has been co-editor of the magazine since the foundation of the ETN Association in 1993.

TextileForum
Postbox 5944
D-30059 Hannover/Germany
Fax: +49-511/813108
E-mail: TFS@ETN-net.org
http://www.ETN-net.org

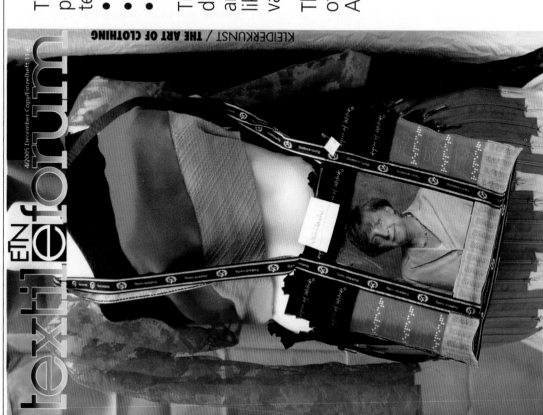

textile forum ETN
4/2005 December Copy/Einzelheft 11€

KLEIDERKUNST / THE ART OF CLOTHING

Letter from the UK Editor

Welcome to Volume 4 of *Textile: The Journal of Cloth & Culture*. This new volume brings some changes, as I am taking a break from the UK Editorship during 2006 to focus on my own research. So I would like to offer a warm welcome to Catherine Harper, who will be replacing me as UK Editor for Volume 4. Catherine is Research Coordinator at University College for the Creative Arts at Epsom. She is an artist and writer, and has contributed to journals, including *Textile*, and is completing a book called *Intersex*.

It's three years since we launched *Textile*, surrounded by over 200 friends and well wishers at the Victoria and Albert Museum in London. We must be doing something right, because in 2005 *Textile* won the ALPSP Charlesworth Award for "Best New Journal." This prestigious award is one of only two given annually by the Association of Learned and Professional Society Publishers and we are very proud to have won. The competition is open to all publishers worldwide for journals launched since 2001 in printed or electronic form. The panel received eighteen applications and considered the content and appearance of each journal, together with the effectiveness of the launch campaign, before declaring *Textile* the winner.

I'd like to take this opportunity to reflect on what we have achieved since the first issue of the Journal, and to look ahead to what we hope to realize in the future. The remit of *Textile: The Journal of Cloth & Culture* remains unique. It aims to bring together research in textiles in an innovative and distinctive academic forum, and to be dynamic, interdisciplinary, international and cutting edge. "Textile" means different things to different people. Here, it refers to a broad-ranging set of critical practices situated within the contexts of visual and material culture, and addressing questions about personal, social and cultural meaning.

We are proud to have published so many important papers on subjects as diverse as "Freud, Fabric and Fetishism," which examined the associations between women, fetishism and cloth; "T-shirts, Testimony and Truth," about the Xhosa women artists in Crossroads, a South African Township; "Domesticating the Floral," tracing the way in which floral cottons imported from India came, by the eighteenth century, to signify Englishness; "Webs of Wrath," on the terrifying power of textile as weapons in ancient Greek mythology; and "Chinese Whispers," exploring the meaning of textile and its relation to the cinematic screen. In addition, *Textile* contributors have critically examined the role of pioneering figures such as the British weaver Ethel Mairet and the US curator Mildred Constantine, and artists such as Narelle Jubelin, Elena Herzog, Mrinalini Mukherjee, Liz Rideal and Gerard Williams. In this short space, it isn't possible to mention all the papers that we

Textile, Volume 4, Issue 1, pp. 5–6
Reprints available directly from the Publishers.
Photocopying permitted by licence only.

have published, but we are grateful to everyone who has contributed to the Journal. *Textile* relies on scholars who submit their work, as well as the generosity of colleagues across the globe who peer-review submissions. Similarly, the Review sections have covered a wide range of books and exhibitions, on both historical and contemporary textiles, with critical evaluation of recent research.

We have also published special issues of the Journal focused on single topics. The first of these, *Digital Dialogues: Textiles and Technology*, was edited by Janis Jefferies and published across two issues. Janis Jefferies stepped down from the UK co-editorship of the Journal in 2003, but has remained active. She is co-editing another special issue, *Shaping Space: Textiles as Architecture and Archaeology*, together with Diana Wood Conroy of the University of Wollongong. A further special issue, this time on *String*, which I will be co-editing with Claire Pajaczkowska of Middlesex University, is also in the pipeline. It is due out in 2007, so there is still time to submit an abstract. If there's an idea that you would like to develop, please contact us by May 1, 2006: p.barnett@gold.ac.uk and c.pajaczkowska@mdx.ac.uk

In 2006, a new section of *Textile* will be introduced. *Dialogue* is for shorter submissions, of between 1,000 and 2,000 words, reflecting current issues and concerns around textile theory and practice. The idea is to promote discussion and debate—so if you'd like to take issue with something published in *Textile*, or if there's an idea or topic you'd like to air, please let the Editors know. *Dialogue* papers can be fully illustrated, or just text. (They are not peer reviewed, but inclusion is subject to editorial decision.)

We hope you will agree that we have accomplished a great deal in terms of taking the subject of textiles forward, but there is much more we would like to do. To help us achieve this aim, we welcome your feedback. Whether or not you would like to submit a paper or article, the Editors would be delighted to hear from you. What do you find useful? What could we do better? While by no means discouraging scholars in the UK, North America, Canada and Australia, I'd like to see the Journal attract more submissions from other parts of the globe, and to develop a more extensive coverage of exhibitions. Tell us about exhibitions that you think should be reviewed. Alternatively, if you have experience in the field and/or in reviewing, and would like to be considered as a contributor to the Exhibition Review section, contact Jennifer Harris, our UK and "rest of the world" exhibitions editor, sending her your CV, and an example of your writing. But please appreciate that *Textile* is only published three times a year, so we can't guarantee to be in print when an exhibition is showing.

I would like to celebrate the hard work of all those who have contributed to *Textile: The Journal of Cloth & Culture*, both in front of, and behind the scenes. Finally, I'd like to thank Catherine Harper for accepting the UK Editorship for Volume 4, and wish her, fellow Editor, Doran Ross and Associate Editor Mary Littrell every success.

Pennina Barnett

Letter from Catherine Harper

I am delighted to be involved with *Textile: The Journal of Cloth & Culture* as UK Editor during 2006, and very much look forward to the year ahead. I would like to thank Pennina Barnett and Jan Gilburt for their inductions to the business of *Textile*, and to wish Pennina all the very best for her busy year of personal research. This New Year has brought several beginnings and endings for me: I have changed roles within the University College for the Creative Arts, becoming Research Coordinator at the Epsom College and relinquishing my previous position running the Textile Design Department. I am in the process of finally completing my book—*Intersex*—which will be published by Berg in 2006. And I have taken on this exciting and challenging role as UK Editor for Volume 4 of *Textile*.

The international profile of *Textile* is significant, and the diversity of papers published within it testifies to the health of what we might think of as general textile culture. I am thrilled and amazed by how many different approaches to considerations of textile come forward from potential contributors, and this reinforces my conviction that the "textile" part of material culture, of visual cultural, of social culture does indeed touch us cradle to grave, and all places in between. The

Journal has established itself as a forum for keen academic scrutiny of textile culture in the broadest and most inclusive of terms, and its high-value content and excellent production values testify to the hard work and dedication of the whole team—Editors and Associate Editor, Review and Exhibitions Editors, Board Members, Editorial Assistants, Publishers and Contributors. Their combined efforts have created a journal of importance, integrity and distinction. As a textile practitioner, writer and academic, I am committed to the critical interrogation of the expansive, expanded and expanding territory we call textile. And, at *Textile*, we seek papers that are part of that interrogation, whether framed through a "textile sensibility" or shaped by other disciplines, other histories and other thought-systems. I look forward very much to this New Year for *Textile: The Journal of Cloth & Culture*, not least to Janis Jefferies' and Diana Wood-Conroy's special issue, and to the introduction of the *Dialogue* section.

I also look forward to questions, comments, conversations, debates—please feel free to contact me at charper@ucreative. ac.uk with any of these.

Catherine Harper

Textile, Volume 4, Issue 1, p. 7
Reprints available directly from the Publishers.
Photocopying permitted by licence only.
© 2006 Berg. Printed in the United Kingdom.

The Aloha Shirt and Ethnicity in Hawaiʻi

Abstract

Hawaii's aloha shirt features brightly colored textiles; this article presents the design evolution of these textiles used in the aloha shirt for each decade from its origin in the 1930s to 2000. Based on a study of over 1,000 shirts and textiles, this study shows that Hawaiian prints and the aloha shirt developed as a result of contributions from several, ethnic groups in multiethnic Hawai'i where there is no ethnic majority. Throughout the decades of the twentieth century, the Hawaiian prints featured in the aloha shirt provided visual testimony to the importance of ethnicity in Hawai'i. This article posits that in a multiethnic society, ethnic dress can function symbolically as a cultural marker representing inclusivity rather than exclusivity. In Hawai'i, the aloha shirt has become a symbol of a pan-ethnic identity and visualy separates insiders from outsiders. To those who live in Hawai'i, it is a visible symbol of their multiethnic heritage.

LINDA B. ARTHUR

Linda B. Arthur is a Professor of Apparel Merchandising and Textiles at Washington State University in the USA. Her research focuses on material culture and the expression of identity, gender, religion, and ethnicity in the dress of cultural groups.

Textile, Volume 4, Issue 1, pp. 8–35
Reprints available directly from the Publishers.
Photocopying permitted by licence only.

The Aloha Shirt and Ethnicity in Hawai'i

Hawai'i, awash in romance, marbled by different cultures, saturated with beauty, and compelling in contrasts, gave birth . . . to the renowned aloha shirt. There is today probably no better known garment in the world that captures a land's "spirit of place." For half a century, the Aloha shirt has been Hawaii's most enduring and visible greeter and ambassador—like a lei, the aloha shirt is worn as a statement of one's love for, and connection to, a most special place.

Tommy Holmes, Quoted in Hope and Tozian, *"The Aloha Shirt"*

Hawaiian textiles in general, and the aloha shirt in particular, have become visible manifestations of the state's multicultural population. In Hawai'i where no one ethnic group is in the majority, a pan-ethnic regional identity, referred to as local identity, can supersede other ethnic identities in the local population. In the case presented here, that regional identity is expressed visually by Hawaiian residents, many of whom wear aloha shirts that showcase numerous ethnic motifs. These shirts are worn in Hawai'i on a daily basis to express multiethnic identities that are tied to a local identity.

In this article, I trace the design evolution of the aloha shirt from its origins in the 1930s to its contemporary use. In doing so, I show that the style lines and design motifs of the aloha shirt developed from the interaction of several immigrant groups. A creole language, Hawaiian pidgin, became integral during this time as a unifying language. In a similar manner, the aloha shirt functions as a creolized garment that brings people of different ethnic backgrounds together, as the garment, and language, assert "local" identity in Hawai'i.

The use of ethnic motifs in aloha shirts is chronicled throughout the twentieth century in order to see the shift in motifs over time. Japanese and Chinese motifs dominated aloha shirt patterns until after the Second World War when they declined in use and Hawaiian motifs, sometimes mixed with Asian motifs, began to dominate. Ethnic motifs continued to be important through the end of the twentieth century, but Hawaiian motifs have continued to represent approximately half of the design motifs used on the aloha shirt. The use of the aloha shirt is a unifying symbol of the aloha spirit, a major theme in Hawai'i representing good will within a diverse and multiethnic community.

Data and Methods

The study of material culture in general, and artifacts in particular, can facilitate new forms and methods of interpretation. Objects, such as dress, can be examined as a form of visual literacy. As Buckridge notes, material culture examined in conjunction with primary historical data widens our view of history and increases the evidence available for interpreting history (Buckridge 2004). Such a combination of methods was found useful in the Hawaiian case study presented here. Hawaiiana in general and the aloha shirt in particular are pop-cultural phenomena that are highly sought by collectors, and finding accurate data on aloha attire was a difficult task before the mid-1990s because materials in print were based on anecdotal writings by collectors. Serious academic research was needed and began at the University of Hawai'i at Manoā in the mid-1990s. By the turn of the century, a few academic articles appeared in the *Clothing and Textiles Research Journal* and three historically accurate books on the topic were published (Irie 1997; Schiffer 1997; Arthur 2000). Most of this work focused on the art and history of the aloha shirt, however none focused on ethnicity in relation to aloha attire, the subject of this article.

Triangulated methods were used in a larger study on the origins of aloha attire[1] that had begun in 1993 and the integration of qualitative and quantitative methods used in examining both primary and secondary sources was found quite useful. Consequently, when the current study on ethnic designs in aloha shirts commenced, the same methodology was employed.

Research for this particular study on the ethnic motifs found in the textiles for Hawaii's aloha shirts began in the late 1990s and was completed in 2002. In order to obtain a thorough cross section of data, and to fully examine the aloha shirt phenomenon, the research involved a triangulated methodology that included both primary and secondary sources. Qualitative methods (extensive interviews with apparel manufacturers), historic data analysis (examination of primary historical records, print materials, photos, and garment analysis), and some quantitative methods (content analysis on data from garment and photo analysis) were interwoven in this research project.

Written primary sources included materials from the archives of aloha shirt manufacturers. Unwritten primary source materials included interviews mentioned above, in addition to analysis of material culture such as an examination of illustrations, ads, and photos. A large sample (2,420) of photographs was briefly examined; only photos with clearly identifiable garment styles were examined in detail, resulting in a final sample size of 1,069 aloha shirt prints. Most of the photos were taken between 1930 and 1999. Using content analysis, design and style features were noted along with the date and photographer, if indicated.

Material culture in the form of extant garments included an examination of 225 aloha shirts; 168 belonged to the CTAHR Historic Costume Collection at the University of Hawai'i at Manoā and the remainder were owned by aloha shirt manufacturers and private collectors in Hawai'i

and California.[2] Dated from 1932 through 2000, these aloha shirts were examined to collect information on both overall style features, and specific design details, such as fabrics, notions, and construction techniques. Provenience for each garment provided additional information as to the socio-historical context. Finally, interviews were conducted with aloha shirt manufacturers, designers, and collectors.

Dress, Symbolism, and Ethnic Identity

Dress is important in social interaction, as noted in the late 1950s by Erving Goffman who stated that dress is a form of non-verbal communication that projects identities. What Goffman understood was that all societies have complex social norms predicated on non-verbal and symbolic behavior (Goffman 1967). Following in Goffman's footsteps, other sociologists have noted that cultural manifestations of ethnicity are also symbolic in nature and work well when they are public and visible; these include language, customs, and dress (Nash 1988; Okamura 1984; Waters 1990). Dress is one of the more noticeable boundary markers used by cultures. Dress is defined as including both body modifications and/or supplements to the body. More specifically, dress includes both body supplements, such as clothing and accessories, and behaviors, such as cosmetic use, plastic surgery, and dieting, as it leads to changes in body shape. Holistically, then, dress functions as an effective means of non-verbal communication during social interaction; it influences the establishment and projection of identity (Eicher and Higgins 1995).

As Eicher notes, the analysis of ethnic dress is quite complex. The ideas behind ethnicity connect to the preservation of an identity for individuals that links to a meaningful heritage. In discussions of ethnicity and identity, controversies have focused on self-definition as opposed to definition by others, and on the fluidity of the concept of ethnicity as individuals move in time and space. Ethnic dress helps to position an individual in time and place relationships. Often the details that distinguish ethnic dress are minute, but they are nevertheless critical for those who claim them as part of their heritage of dress. Sometimes what appears as ethnic dress may seem quaint and picturesque as it appeals to tourists (Eicher 1995).

Numerous case studies of ethnic dress show that it is a highly salient marker of group belonging and can represent national, regional, and ethnic identities (Lenz 1995; Lynch 1995; Welters 1995). Similarly, ethnographic studies of dress as an expression of ethnic identity show that when ethnic groups live within larger, more dominant groups, ethnic dress can function as a cultural boundary marker, presenting and affirming the exclusiveness of ethnic identity (Carrel 1999; Daly 1999; Graybill and Arthur 1999; Renee 2000; Shirazi 2000; Stimpfl 2000).

Most of the research on ethnic dress and identity shows dress as a cultural boundary marker of exclusivity. Of relevance to this study, Welters examined ethnic dress in Greece, and noted that when a community is composed of mixed heritage, it is necessary to consider the concept of dressing to represent ethnic identity while it simultaneously signifies cultural affiliation (Welters 1995). This article posits that in a multiethnic society, such as Hawai'i, ethnic dress can function symbolically as a cultural marker representing the larger cultural value of embracing ethnic differences; in this case study then, ethnic dress represents inclusivity rather than exclusivity.

Although dress has been sometimes considered a code to be deciphered, and some notable authors have compared the metaphor of dress to language (Barthes 1983; Bogatyrev 1971; Lurie 2000; Turner 1980), to do so is risky. Dress does not have grammar and syntax, and it cannot be decoded in a one-to-one comparison like a true code (McCracken 1987). Clothing is able to project multiple meanings simultaneously and in a visual manner. This is not to say that there are no similarities to language; in this case study of Hawaiian material culture, I will draw comparisons between the development of a creole language (Hawaiian pidgin) that allowed people from varied ethnicities to communicate orally in Hawai'i, and a similar development of a creolized garment, the aloha shirt, as a visual manifestation of a pan-ethnic identity in Hawai'i. First however, we must examine the complex issue of ethnicity in Hawai'i.

Ethnicity in Hawai'i is very salient. People in Hawai'i identify themselves in two ways, as a member of one or more ethnic groups, and as "local," meaning that they are from Hawai'i, but may not be Hawaiian by race. Being local in Hawai'i generally means one is *kama'aina*, and emotionally invested in Hawai'i as a multiethnic society. Despite the passage of time and the effects of acculturation, many people celebrate their multiple ethnic heritages. "Local" identity is expressed in a number of ways, from wearing Hawaii's aloha attire to speaking Hawaiian pidgin (Brown and Arthur 2003).

Ethnicity in Hawai'i

An ethnic group is a collectivity of people who share normative patterns within a larger population, and interact with people in other collectives within the larger social system. Ethnicity is defined as the degree of conformity to the shared norms shown by members of the collectivity (Cohen 1974). Ethnic identity is a self-constructed understanding of one's cultural and ethnic background and includes an internalization of the meaning and implications of that group membership. The development of an ethnic identity takes place through a process of exploration and commitment over time (Phinney 2005).

In Hawai'i, ethnicity was not an issue when the nineteenth century opened, because the population was composed entirely of Hawaiians. However, with the arrival of Westerners and their diseases, the Hawaiian population was decimated. As plantations developed, the need for labor was met by importing workers,

primarily from Asia. Chinese immigration began in the 1850s, followed by the Portuguese in the late 1870s, Japanese in the late 1880s, and Koreans and Filipinos after 1900. By 1959 when Hawai'i became the fiftieth US state, only a tenth of the population in the Hawaiian Islands was ethnically Hawaiian (Arthur 2000).

Hawaii's population today is primarily Asian, and Asian-American identity is a category better seen as a mixed race or ethnic category. In Hawai'i, the population is multiethnic (Cheng 2004) because it has been transformed by interracial marriages which have led to the extraordinary ethnic diversity seen in Hawai'i today. Okamura examined this issue and noted that the rate of interracial marriage in Hawai'i has tripled in this century to 34% of all marriages. As a consequence of immigration and intermarriage, no one ethnic group is in the majority; a large portion of Hawaii's residents claim two or more ethnic identities. The largest ethnic groups are Caucasian (24%), Japanese (20%), Hawaiian and part-Hawaiian (19%), Filipino (11%), and Chinese (5%) (Cheng and Linh Ho 2003; Okamura 1984).

Due to the perception of ethnic harmony resulting from racial integration, Hawai'i was considered to be an example of ethnic harmony by the Chicago School of sociology in the early part of this century. Robert Park, a notable member of this group of scholars, taught at the University of Hawai'i, and in an article (published in 1926) used Hawai'i as a model of what the United States could achieve (quoted in

Haas 1994). However, the utopian ideal of ethnic harmony has not resulted, although according to Kirkpatrick more tolerance does exist in Hawai'i than on the US mainland. The aloha spirit, which maintains that interaction between individuals should occur without reference to ethnic prejudice, is part of the public code of ethnic relationships in Hawai'i. The danger in idealizing ethnic interactions is that glossing over this issue can hide negative interracial relations (Haas 1994; Kirkpatrick 1987).

As Okamura has shown, though most of the people in Hawai'i have Asian roots, they do not identify themselves as Asian Americans. They tend to self-identify with the Asian country of origin, at the same time claiming a pan-ethnic identity referred to as "local" identity. Based on the opposition between locals and people considered non-local, such as recent immigrants, the military, and tourists, local identity provides for symbolic boundaries between groups. Of significance to this study, local identity was well-established before the 1960s (Okamura 1984).

In Hawai'i, the population is primarily differentiated by the length of time they have been in the islands. *Kama'aina* are "locals"; the term means old-timers, and refers to people who were born in Hawai'i, regardless of ethnic identification. *Malihini* means newcomers, and refers to those who live in the islands but were not born in Hawai'i. A third and economically important group are the tourists, who usually wear aloha shirts, but are unaware of the meanings related to ethnicity.

Retaining ethnic heritage is consistent with the notion of multiculturalism or cultural pluralism. This perspective holds that subcultures manage to resist total acculturation, and intentionally maintain their ethnic cultural practices while functioning within the dominant society. Some intergenerational studies involving various ethnic groups in the US and Canada showed that, despite the acculturation achieved by ethnic individuals, some degree of identification with the ethnic culture persists through generations. That is, although some loss of the original ethnic identity inevitably occurs during the process of acculturation, the intensity of ethnic identification does not diminish in a linear fashion over the generations (Jeffres 2000; Laroche *et al.* 1998).

Markers of Local Identity: Language and Aloha Shirts

Creole communities developed in the Americas, Asia, and Africa, and led to mixed racial groups that became visible social groups. Early on, creole communities developed symbolic markers. Creole languages have a capacity for generating imagined communities, building in effect *particular solidarities* (Anderson 1996).

The creole language known as Hawaiian pidgin originated as a form of communication on the plantations in Hawai'i when numerous people of various ethnicities were brought in to work in Hawai'i. it has been influenced by many languages, including Portuguese, Hawaiian, Cantonese, Japanese, Filipino, and Korean and Spanish as spoken by Puerto Ricans in Hawai'i. Outside the plantations, pidgin began to be used in the schools and it became the primary language of most people in Hawaii in the nineteenth century. Today, most people born or raised in Hawaii can speak and understand pidgin to some extent. Knowledge of pidgin is an important requirement for doing business in Hawai'i. Today, Hawaiian pidgin functions symbolically as a means of identifying locals from outsiders. Similarly, in Hawai'i the wearing of aloha shirts may identify people as *kama'aina*, or, more particularly in the current times, locals can be differentiated from tourists based on the particular style of shirts worn.

Textile prints may have, like creole language, been a (visual) testimony to pluralism and the need to celebrate ethnic differences but within a pan-ethnic visual medium called the aloha shirt.

Precursors to the Aloha Shirt

Shirts came into Hawai'i with the whaling and sandalwood trades, in the late eighteenth and early nineteenth centuries. Sailors landing in the Islands wore loose-fitting, long-sleeved upper garments called frocks. The Hawaiians transliterated the word "frock" into "*palaka.*" Heavy cotton fabrics were also imported; a plaid which became known as *palaka* is a heavy cotton cloth woven in a white and dark-blue plaid design. Soon the term was used to define not the shirt, but the fabric. By the end of the nineteenth century, as immigrants came to Hawai'i and worked in the fields and mills,

Figure 1
Courtesy of DeSoto Brown. In Figure 1 we see a group of people at a party in the 1950s; most are kama'aina of Asian ancestries. The men wear aloha shirts, and the women wear holomu'u and mu'umu'u. Most of the garments feature prints with ethnic features.

the use of *palaka* spread because of its durability, coolness, and design. Tailored shirts with collars and buttons up the front had already been brought into Hawai'i by American businessmen and served as design inspiration for *palaka* shirts and jackets; these were more closely fitting garments than the frock shirt. *Palaka* shirts were commonly worn by plantation workers of Portuguese and Hawaiian ancestry. The *palaka* shirt was mass-produced for plantation laborers along with work clothes and uniforms beginning in 1922. By this time the Filipino man's shirt called the *barong tagalog*—a sheer, cool long-sleeved shirt worn loose over trousers—was worn in Hawai'i. Chinese, Japanese, and Euro-American custom tailors were busy in the Islands, and had ready access to fabrics, most of

which were imported from Japan. Printed cottons with Asian motifs were used most commonly in addition to Japanese resist-dyed ikats known as *yukata* cloth. Silks were also used; both raw silk and finely woven silks were also imported from Japan. Such fabrics were used for both Western-styled clothing and kimono. The stage was set for all these multiethnic forces to blend together and create what would become the aloha shirt, a garment that has come to represent the multiethnic community of Hawai'i.

While most clothing in early twentieth-century Hawai'i was made at home, production of clothing by custom tailors, like Musa-Shiya the Shirtmaker, began with men's Western-styled shirts as well as kimono, *hapi* coats, and other Asian-styled garments.

Almost all the garments produced in the 1920s were made of silk or cotton.

Proto-Hawaiian Design
The 1930s through the end of the Second World War was a period of transition in Hawaiian textile design. The transition resulted from both the availability of imported goods (primarily from Asia) to a changing sense of identity of the population. The ethnic mix, which had begun with the importation of laborers in the previous century, had started to stabilize through both necessity and intermarriage. The different ethnicities began to come together to redefine what it meant to be Hawaiian, based on culture and a sense of place, rather than genealogy. This sense of cooperation came out of the

Figure 2
1930s cotton *yukata* print fabric, generally used for casual kimono, used in an early aloha shirt.

necessity of living under the plantation's oppressive conditions. The plantation economy dominated Hawai'i until after the Second World War and the ramifications of this economic system permeated life on the Islands. The class differences that resulted from the plantation economy were also manifested in clothing. There was an enormous disparity between the upper class, which was primarily composed of white businessmen and their families, as well as *kama'aina* families—the descendants of the early white settlers. In terms of population, the vast majority of the people in Hawai'i were on the lower end of the socio-economic scale. Native Hawaiians were not privy to the economic growth of the times, nor were the plantation workers (who were primarily immigrants) and their descendants.

The beginning of tourism as a major Hawaiian industry coupled with the increase of US military personnel stationed in Hawai'i led to a global awareness of Hawai'i. By the 1930s the promotional efforts of the Hawai'i Tourist Bureau, already in existence for thirty years, were focused on promoting the Territory as a colorful, romantic tourist destination. The intense color found in the Islands' fish and flowers was hyped in the promotional literature that was already abundant by the 1930s. Flowers were praised continually, and the stage was set for the depiction of Hawaiian flora and fauna on the textiles produced in the next decade.

To understand the development of the aloha shirt, one must first understand what textiles were in use in Hawai'i prior to the end of the Second World War. Plain cotton broadcloth was, by far, the dominant fabric for all garments, from the holokū, mu'umu'u, and kimono, to the aloha shirt. These were done in lightweight cotton fabrics, such as Japanese yukata cloth, with figures and flora on a blue or black background being the most popular.[7] Silk, kabe crepe, and challis (usually a fine wool) were used for dressier shirts or women's garments. Undergarments were made either of fine silk, for the upper classes, or lightweight rayon, for the lower classes. This rayon was much like today's nylon tricot, often found in underwear. It was unsuitable for printing and did not have the strength and texture necessary to retain vivid color. (It was not until the 1940s that a heavier rayon was developed and could hold color.) The early aloha shirts were made with kimono fabrics of silk or kabe crepe, or of simple cotton broadcloth two-color prints. Some screen printing occurred in the 1930s, although most fabrics were imported from Japan. The design motifs on the early 1930s aloha

shirts were generally Japanese or Chinese and applied to the greige goods by roller printing in Japan.[8]

Raw silk was occasionally used for garments, and along with a heavy cotton, was also used for draperies in the 1930s. Photos in Hawaiian museum archives show people (even celebrities like Bing Crosby) in Hawai'i wearing cotton shirts with predominantly Japanese motifs in the early 1930s; from the content analysis of 1,091 photos, in the 1930s, 44% of the aloha shirts had Japanese motifs, compared to 12% with Chinese motifs, and 23% with Hawaiian motifs (see Table 1). By the mid-1930s, tropical floral motifs appeared, but these were on long-sleeved shirts made with drapery fabric remnants. At about the same time two-color broadcloth prints appear with Hawaiian words; these designs resemble stickers put on luggage during this era. The earliest photos of prints with Hawaiian floral motifs on fabric designed for apparel are from 1937; these prints were on cotton fabrics of various weights.[9]

In 1936, a pivotal year, two major garment manufacturers, Kamehameha and Branfleet, set up factories in order to produce sportswear, and the term "aloha shirt" was trademarked by Ellery Chun. While sales to the local population were sluggish, the major markets for aloha shirts were tourists in Hawai'i , and consumers on the US mainland. The clothing needs of Hawaiian residents were focused on work clothing, due to economics. Hawai'i was still a plantation economy, with the bulk of its population primarily in the lower classes. Only the upper classes could afford clothing

for leisure activities: "It was the Depression, then, and still Plantation days. I didn't know anyone who could afford aloha shirts when they first came out, and my family wasn't poor like most," said a Chinese-American gentleman.[10]

During the Christmas season of 1936, a shipping strike caused the fabric to be stranded in California with the finished garments in Hawai'i. The companies tried to sell the garments in Hawai'i but the locals did not buy the shirts. At that time, the population was conservative and dressed formally, following the styles of the US mainland. Their choice of clothing in the 1930s was due to assimilation. Ethnic identity was suppressed as the Territory of Hawai'i was Westernizing. Other than on the plantations, people gave up ethnic dress in favor of imported American clothing. The focus was not yet on a local identity. As a consequence, there was not yet a local market for aloha shirts, so the fledgling apparel industry began exporting aloha attire; only 5% of their garments were sold locally. "In 1939 Kamehameha produced twenty-three exclusive print designs ... all of the cottons being printed on the US mainland" (Arlen 1939). Branfleet (later renamed Kahala Sportswear) was also founded in 1936, like Kamehameha; Kahala is one of the oldest and largest firms in the Islands; both companies began by selling aloha shirts made of kabe crepes, in Asian designs.

Branfleet, Kamehameha, and Shaheen were the first Hawaiian apparel companies to supply sportswear to the US mainland on

Figure 3
Hawaiian tourist print on early aloha shirt, dated 1937.

a large scale. By 1939, the most popular prints were still quite subtle with small motifs and little color contrast. These basic designs with slight modifications were used through the end of the Second World War (Laughlin n.d.).

Tourism continued to grow, and that unique demand led to the development of the Royal Hawaiian Manufacturing Company, founded in 1937 by Max Lewis. Motifs on the early Royal Hawaiian aloha shirts tended to be very bold

Hawaiian designs. Lewis focused on the production of clothing for sale to tourists, and some of the earliest proto-Hawaiian shirts (with labels), come from Royal Hawaiian Manufacturing.

The Aloha Shirt

While the predecessors of the Hawaiian shirt were established by the mid-1930s, what is recognized around the world as the early Hawaiian shirt—the brightly patterned rayons with Hawaiian

Table 1 Ethnic design motifs printed on a sample of aloha shirts

	WES	IND	JAP	CHI	HAW	SE/A	POLY	H/A	H/P	Total
1930s, raw score	6	0	23	6	12	2	2	1	0	52
percentages	12%	0%	44%	12%	23%	4%	4%	2%	0%	
1940s, raw score	3	0	37	31	119	3	8	3	4	208
percentages	1%	0%	18%	15%	57%	1%	4%	1%	2%	
1950s, raw score	4	1	40	29	291	23	32	7	10	437
percentages	1%	0%	9%	7%	67%	5%	7%	2%	2%	
1960s, raw score	9	3	17	8	61	6	16	3	15	138
percentages	7%	2%	12%	6%	44%	4%	12%	2%	11%	
1970s, raw score	9	4	10	0	37	2	6	0	5	73
percentages	12%	5%	14%	0%	51%	3%	8%	0%	7%	
1980s, raw score	15	1	4	2	46	0	7	0	3	78
percentages	19%	1%	5%	3%	59%	0%	9%	0%	4%	
1990s, raw score	0	1	22	10	40	10	0	0	0	83
percentages	0%	1%	27%	12%	48%	12%	0%	0%	0%	
totals	46	10	153	86	606	46	71	14	37	1069
	4%	1%	14%	8%	57%	4%	7%	1%	3%	

Legend

WES – Western CHI – Chinese POLY – Polynesian
IND – Indian HAW – Hawaiian H/A – Hawaiian and Asian
JAP – Japanese SE/A – Southeast Asian H/P – Hawaiian and Polynesian

motifs—was created *after* the Second World War. Hawaiian motifs did not appear on the early aloha shirts until just before the beginning of the war, which seriously disrupted the fledgling aloha shirt industry. At that time, most retailers sold shirts made either in cottons or *kabe* crepe, and most had Asian design motifs. The *kabe* crepe shirts were far and away the most colorful. These shirts were reported to have been made by Japanese mothers out of silk and crepe kimono fabric scraps for their schoolchildren. Similarly, reports exist that boys from an upper-class private school began having shirts custom made from bright kimono fabric to wear for special activities. Yet another common explanation has been that families had matching shirts made of bright kimono fabrics for special events.

In the mid-1930s the word "aloha" was attached to many types of merchandise—there were "aloha" tea sets and "aloha" coasters, so the term was not originally used for sportswear. The first to use the term in ads was Musa-Shiya the Shirtmaker who advertised in 1935 in the *Honolulu Advertiser* on June 28, 1935: "Aloha shirts—well tailored, beautiful designs and radiant colors." However, as we saw above, it was Ellery Chun who trademarked the term "aloha shirt" in 1936. He too began by selling shirts made of traditional kimono fabrics,

Figure 4
1930s aloha shirt made of Japanese *kabe* crepe usually used for girl's kimono.

although he wanted to produce an expressly Hawaiian shirt. He commissioned artists (notably his sister, Ethyl Lum) to create Hawaiian designs of local flowers and fish, and had these designs printed on *kabe* crepe. Because they sold well, Chun noted that: "In 1936 I figured it was a good idea to own the trademark" (Moor 1978).

After the Japanese attacked Pearl Harbor, Hawaii, and the US entered the Second World War, Japanese motifs on aloha shirts fell out of favor and reduced significantly to only 18% during this time period, while Chinese motifs increased to 15% and Hawaiian motifs more than doubled to 57% (see Table 1). Since there was a large population of ethnic Japanese in Hawaii at the time, it was important for the Japanese-American population to show their allegiance to Hawaii and the US. Figure 5 illustrates this: Mitsuru Doi was the first Japanese American to join the Army in 1943;

here he prepares to leave home for his swearing-in ceremony wearing an aloha shirt that featured a map of the Hawaiian Islands.

Shipping between Hawai'i and the US was curtailed during the Second World War and this prepared the way for an industry which could no longer import or export garments. Fabrics had to be printed locally. Due to the scarcity of imported Western-styled clothing, aloha attire became more popular on the Islands for the local population. For some time, tourists and military personnel had readily adopted the bold aloha shirts, and the islanders began to wear aloha shirts en masse.

The Post-War 1940s to Mid-1950s: Classic Silkies

After textile imports ceased during the Second World War the creation of uniquely Hawaiian textiles in very bold prints dominated aloha shirts. Artists began designing textiles with tropical motifs such as Hawaii's beautiful flowers, bright fish, and tropical scenes. Introduced in the late 1930s, drapery shirts were among the earliest tropical print aloha shirts. Historical motifs were added to the designs as well. Consequently the bright, bold rayon aloha shirts, known to collectors around the world as Hawaiian shirts, originated in the late 1940s. The brightly patterned rayon aloha shirt became famous throughout the nation as servicemen returned home from Hawai'i, and as tourism increased through the mid-twentieth century. The 1940s and 1950s were the heyday of Hawaiian tourism; fabrics with Hawaiian motifs were used extensively in aloha shirts both for sale to tourists and to the Hawaiian-born population.[11]

Several of the manufacturers in the pre-war period avoided using rayon because, as one noted "The rayon was garbage .... It was flimsy and inexpensive ... after the war, they came out with rayon that was heavier, and it finally held the dyes. Rayon shirts with a smooth finish and Hawaiian prints were only seen after the Second World War. No one was printing that stuff before the war" (Wentzel 1989).[12]

The heavy rayon fabrics described above felt like silk, hence the nickname, "silkies." These shirts had bold colors and brilliant tropical designs, often done in "hash" prints or "chop suey" prints—where assorted motifs, often of mixed ethnic backgrounds, were randomly thrown onto a fabric. One designer said that this was similar to the mixed-ethnic population. The Hawaiian prints continued to dominate during the 1950s, with 67% of the sample, while Japanese (9%) and Chinese prints (7%) declined significantly (see Table 1).

Hawaiian textile art, especially the most outrageously designed, has been appreciated by

Figure 5
Mitsuru Doi leaves Hawaii to join the US Army, 1943: Courtesy of US Library of Congress.

connoisseurs for several decades. A few artists produced huge designs in which the entire shirt was treated like a canvas. Some of these featured air-brushed designs of Polynesian maidens. Tourism created a ready market for more adventurous aloha attire by the post-Second World War era. Designs grew more daring, incorporating such uniquely Pacific patterns as palm trees, hula girls, Diamond Head, the Aloha Tower, surfers, and pineapples. Color combinations were no longer staid: colors became riotous. Textile designers studied the art and artifacts in museums all over Asia and the Pacific region, and this influence was incorporated into Hawaiian textile design.

Alfred Shaheen, a pioneering apparel manufacturer in Hawai'i, stated that he and his textile artists wanted to "create a textile design that had some meaning to it ... we put in more substance into the design, and on the hangtag we'd write the story behind the design.[13]

Similarly, John Meigs created designs imbued with ethnic meanings. He also created designs under his Hawaiian name, Keoni. Meig's textile designs for aloha shirts were based on aspects of Hawaiian culture, flora, and marine life from the late 1940s through 1951, and foreshadowed the beginnings of abstract art in Hawaiian textile design.[14]

By the late 1950s, rayon was no longer being used in aloha attire. This was obvious from the number of well-documented aloha shirts in the University's historic costume collection, but was clarified by Shaheen who stated: "The idea that they quit using rayon due to

Figure 7
Alfred Shaheen and Tony Walker (center) meet with designers in late 1950s. Courtesy of Camille Shaheen Tunberg.

a fire at du Pont is a myth. Rayon became old hat—it simply went out of style. Period." The gaudy floral designs were considered too garish and were no longer fashionable. Funderburke noted that cotton was consistently the primary fabric used for Hawaiian apparel (Funderburke 1965). In the late 1950s blended fabrics of cotton and arnel came into being and the promise of permanent press fabrics brought cottons with synthetic blends into style.

In the late 1940s and early 1950s, major retail stores on the US mainland promoted Hawaiian-made garments. Filene's of Boston claimed to have had "the largest exhibit of Hawaiian material ever assembled outside the islands." This kind of attention, coupled with the introduction of air traffic between Hawai'i and

Figure 8
Cotton yardage from Shaheen. 1950s.

the US mainland resulted in the air transport of garments from Kamehameha and Kahala to Boston via Pan American World Airways and American Airlines. Several garment companies began producing Aloha shirts in the 1940s for both the local Hawaiian and American markets.

The aloha shirt became the ultimate picture postcard representing exotic, tropical vacations on the Islands. Out-of-towners continued to make up a large part of the buying public until the Second World War when exports were halted. Locals bought the shirts to support the economy, and members of the armed forces who were stationed in Hawai'i snatched up dozens of the colorful keepsakes during their tenure in the tropics. President Harry Truman and entertainer Arthur Godfrey made public appearances in aloha shirts, stimulating their popularity.

Apparel manufacturers generally bought their fabric from the US mainland, but these textile companies required runs of at least 10,000 yards. Japanese mills had minimum runs of just 3,000 yards, so until the war, Hawaiian manufacturers often obtained yardage from Japan. The cessation of imports and exports during the Second World War created drastic changes in the aloha shirt industry. Alfred Shaheen noted:

During the war there was one or two million servicemen in Hawai'i who were introduced to the Islands. Some stayed and married, others went home and then came back with wives. They introduced the aloha shirt to the US mainland ... This was about 1950 when tourism started to be important. We weren't a tourist market yet because there were only three or four hotels then. There was a craze for Hawai'i on the US mainland then, related to the push for statehood in the US Congress.

The aloha shirt became a hot commodity and travelers often took aloha shirts home with them. Textile designs included words in the Hawaiian language, historical sites, flowers, and cultural motifs. Kamehameha Garment Company accomplished an impressive feat in 1951 by producing the seven-color reproduction of the Eugene Savage Matson menu painting for prints on sportswear. With the movie *From Here to Eternity* aloha shirts exploded on the fashion scene since the actors were dressed in aloha shirts, and many other films set in Hawai'i followed. Through this visual medium, the bright, bold aloha shirts were taken into towns throughout the United States.

Aloha shirts were still seen as casual dress in Hawai'i, and were not considered appropriate for the business world until after the Second World War. Aloha Week brought about change. Until then, men in Hawai'i wore plain shirts with ties to work. There was a lot of resistance to wearing aloha shirts for anything but casual wear. In 1954, some local businesses began to encourage broader use of the aloha shirt. Employees were asked to wear aloha shirts throughout the humid summer, but cautioned that they be "clean and tucked-in." The editor of the newspaper expressed hope that other businessmen

Figure 9
Rayon shirt, produced in the early
1950s by Duke Kahanamoku. Worn
in the film *From Here to Eternity*.
Courtesy of Richard Smith.

would join in wearing local attire (Wentzel 1989: 57).

The 1950s reflected a constant push toward Westernization in Hawai'i; after half a century as an American territory, Hawai'i ended the decade by becoming a state in 1959. During this time, the garment manufacturing industry nearly tripled sales due to the increased national interest in Hawai'i. Sales promotions by national and local manufacturers pushed casual wear in conjunction with the growth of suburban living, and the growing tourist trade was just about to take off as the construction of several hotels led to a dramatic increase in tourism.[15] The exoticism of Hawai'i captured the nation's imagination.

Movies had a huge impact with at least one blockbuster per year set in the Islands. Hawai'i became a state on August 21, 1959 after several years of promotion in the US Congress. As a result of the constant media attention, the years just before and after 1959 represented a time when Hawai'i had the nation's attention. "[A]loha shirts became a whole way of dressing" according to Alfred Shaheen.

In the late 1950s, a renewed interest in items of local material culture was seen in textile design.[16] Local textile artists, most of whom were of Japanese descent, studied artifacts and incorporated imagery from them into textile design. By the 1960s, aloha shirts were in great demand by local consumers. While at first that demand was for aloha shirts for local people to wear to ethnic and Hawaiian festivals, over time people in Hawai'i began to wear aloha attire more frequently. Manufacturers found this to be a positive move, in that they had begun to fear that conventional US mainland modes of dress might supplant island garb (Green 1985: 13). Textile designers such as Bob Sato, who worked for Alfred Shaheen, focused on Japanese and Chinese designs (see Figure 10).

Sato was a fine artist, and his impact was felt in that the percentages of Japanese designs increased to 12% of the sample in the 1960s. Other fine textile artists like Elsie Krassas also had an impact. She focused on Hawaiian and Polynesian tropical prints and created bold tropical textiles; designing for movie stars made her famous. The percentage of Hawaiian prints declined a bit from the earlier period (44%), but her work increased the popularity of Polynesian designs, which hit an all-time high of 12% of the sample (see Table 1).[17] Textile designers went to Tahiti and other locations to study the material culture of Polynesian islands. From this exposure, they

Figure 10
Rice Bowls and Chopsticks; cotton. Produced by Alfred Shaheen, 1956. Courtesy of Camille Shaheen Tunberg.

Figure 11
Polynesian *tapa* print, cotton
barkcloth. Deone's Sportswear. 1970s.

created designs with Polynesian elements and stimulated a trend for Polynesian-inspired textiles that continues to this day.

After Hawai'i became a US state in 1959, it was clear that there was a reciprocal relationship between Hawai'i and the US mainland. Movies continued to be made about Hawai'i, and began to focus on surfing, historically the sport of Hawaiian kings. This sport became popular on the US mainland, particularly in California, as a result of the passion with which it was accepted by visitors to Hawai'i, particularly the military and tourists. As they returned home to the US mainland from Hawai'i, they brought both the sport of surfing, and its requisite aloha shirt, into focus in California. The aloha shirt became associated in California with being young and

hip, and wearing Hawaiian shirts in suburban high schools and colleges became a fad that led to a more casual style of dress overall. "By the late 1960s, informality of dress became something of a civil right" (Kane 1986).

In 1962 The Hawaiian Fashion Guild staged "Operation Liberation"—an attempt to encourage acceptance of printed aloha wear for business attire. A Senate resolution was passed urging the regular use of Aloha attire from Lei Day (May Day) throughout the summer. Hawaii's apparel manufacturers launched a campaign to institute Aloha Friday within the business community, encouraging employers to allow aloha attire to be worn to work every Friday. Aloha Friday officially commenced in 1966.[18] By the end of the decade the aloha shirt had

become accepted as business dress in Hawai'i. The young men who started the fad of wearing aloha shirts in California in the 1960s ended up in positions of power in California and were able to push for a more casual style of dress in California offices, at least on Fridays. Today's Casual Fridays in American corporations began as an offshoot of Hawaii's Aloha Fridays (Arthur 2000).

During the 1960s, aloha shirt design evolved into two different streams. Tourists continued to favor the bold and brightly colored designs that were made popular in the 1950s. However, for local use, people in Hawaii favored more muted designs to wear for business. The fabrics seen in aloha attire in the early 1960s tended to favor subtle designs with regular repeats. The use of Hawaiian motifs decreased in favor of a wider diversity of ethnic motifs, many of which were scaled down in size. The major innovation of the 1960s was the use of reverse prints in aloha shirts. Often called "inside out shirts," the back side of the fabric was intentionally used as the right side of the fabric on aloha shirts. Faded shirts were a mark of local identity, and were used to differentiate locals from tourists. The reverse print shirt was created to mimic the look of the faded aloha shirts so beloved by surfers.

The 1970s: Ethnicity Celebrated

All over America in the 1970s, we were fascinated by ethnicity and focused on it in numerous ways. People "got in touch" with their ethnic origins, and discovered the beauty of traditional arts and crafts from cultures all over the world. The celebration of ethnic difference was seen in clothing as well as other forms of material culture. For the previous decade, aloha attire looked like American dress with Hawaiian fabrics; in the late 1970s the Hawaiian garment designers drew their inspiration from all over the globe.[19]

Ethnicity continued as an integrating idea throughout this decade. In the latter half of the 1970s Hawai'i refocused on its own cultural history. There was a new attention paid to the traditional crafts and practices of Hawaiian culture. The Hokule'a, a replica of the early Hawaiian voyaging canoes, had its first long-distance voyage in 1975; this stimulated Hawaiian imaginations and led to a resurgence in Hawaiian craft production, which set the stage for what would be termed "The

Hawaiian Renaissance." The renewed focus on Hawaiiana was seen in the sample of aloha shirt prints studied (see Table 1).

Celebration of cultural diversity in aloha attire went beyond the incorporation of design details from other cultures, to wholesale adoption of fabrics from other cultures. Batik fabrics from Indonesia were very popular in aloha shirts and *mu'umu'u*; *kente* cloth, *dashiki* prints, and batiks from Africa were used in *mu'umu'u*. Chinese brocades and Thai silks were popular in *holoku*- as well as silk blend fabrics that simulated the Philippines' traditional *piña* cloth made from pineapple fiber. These fabrics were used in all forms of aloha attire in the early 1970s.

By the late 1970s, there was a clear trend regarding aloha shirts: those worn by Hawaiian residents were usually more subdued than aloha shirts worn by tourists. The favored designs were Hawaiian in nature followed by Japanese motifs (see Table 1). The use of aloha shirts in the workplace became accepted practice, so long as the shirts had simple designs with regular repeats. The boldly patterned fabrics were considered a bit too shocking for the business world, and a compromise was made with reverse prints. Softer colors were used for business shirts, as opposed to casual aloha shirts. Since casual shirts in Hawai'i had generally been worn loose over the trousers, during the shift of aloha shirts into a business environment in the 1970s, there was much discussion as to the appropriate way to wear aloha shirts at the office. Eventually, the

Figure 12
Primo beer shirt; cotton barkcloth by
Go Barefoot. 1970s.

standard practice adopted was to wear the shirts tucked in. However, this has changed in recent years to less formality in Hawaiian offices, and the shirts can be worn either way, depending upon the nature and composition of the business.

The Hawaiian Renaissance began in the late 1970s and continues today; it started as the local population began a renewed appreciation of Hawaiian material culture. Traditional Hawaiian designs from *kapa* to the chop suey prints of the 1940s and 1950s returned to dominate aloha wear design, done on both rayons and synthetics. Cottons once again were fashionable and a variety of ethnic design motifs appeared on aloha shirts. However, again, Hawaiian designs dominated, and a favorite print featured Primo Beer, the only locally owned Hawaiian beer company. This shirt, in addition to the *palaka* aloha shirt, became symbolic of local identity (see Figure 12).

In the late 1970s, designers began to reproduce the classic "silkies." Reproductions have dominated the aloha shirt industry through the end of the century:

Colorful Hawaiian prints from territorial days are being used not only for men's aloha shirts but for women's blouses, *jackets, dresses and shorts as well. Imprinted with island motifs—pineapples, surfers, tropical flowers, hula girls, ukuleles, steamships and coconut palms—silkies are executed in the art deco style ... Fashionable Honolulu men's stores began to stock real "antique" shirts and when vintage shirts ran out, manufacturers "dusted off history" and the recreations came off the line. (Dickson 1979)*

As part of the Hawaiian Renaissance, Hawaiian quilting was also a form of material culture that was rediscovered.

Hawaiian quilt motifs began to appear on apparel in the late 1970s and continue to be a major form of design inspiration today. Frequently custom-made clothing with appliqué of Hawaiian quilt designs will be ordered for a family having a special event. While the whole family may have matching aloha shirts or *mu'umu'u*, more frequently the appliqué designs are consistent but colors vary and are coordinated around a color theme. Major events include the baby luau, weddings, graduations, hula performances, and other major celebrations where the family comes together. Having custom-made aloha attire created for an event is extremely expensive, and many families will just wear ordinary aloha attire to family events.

Aloha attire provides for a unifying element that suppresses ethnic differences within the family. Since most families have members from varied ethnic groups, aloha attire is used to provide for an element of group consensus, as one woman noted:

Although I'm Japanese and Haole [white], we have Koreans, Hawaiians, and Chinese in our family. If Auntie Reiko came to a family gathering in kimono, Auntie Grace came in a cheong sam, and Auntie Soyoung came in hanbok, we'd have a real problem! Though most of us are local and grew up here, the politics of the past can always be there under the surface. We strive for ho'okipa [hospitable conduct] and lokahi [harmony]. So we intentionally are careful with how we dress. Like most of us here in Hawai'i, we're a multiethnic family and there's no better way to show that than wearing aloha attire.

Aloha shirts came into international consciousness by the 1980s when simple designs were considered boring, and in the haute couture salons of Europe nostalgia reigned supreme. Yves St Laurent and Kenzo Okada brought out lines of clothing based on Tahitian prints. Fashion directors returned from the fashion showings in Europe ready for the new look. Dave Rochlen, from Surf Line Hawai'i, noted that "their renaissance began in Europe. The Art Deco movement was important and this came together with a renewed willingness to revisit ... the European concept of Polynesia as Paradise" (quoted in Rampell 1999). In Hawaii, more Western motifs appeared on aloha shirts (19%), and Hawaiian motifs reached 59% of the sample (see Table 1).

As the 1990s began, the quality of rayon had improved and polyester (which had been used for about fifteen years) went out of favor as it did not sell as well in the Islands due to its lack of breathability. Ethnic motifs increased in importance in aloha shirt prints: Japanese prints accounted for 27%, Chinese 12%, Southeast Asian 12%, and Hawaiian motifs dropped to 48% (see Table 1). Nonetheless, several designers put their reputations on the line and went back to the traditional Hawaiian prints of the post-war period. They brought out the "new" silkies that looked surprisingly like the original silkies of the late 1940s and 1950s. Since this time, these vintage reproductions have dominated the market in Hawai'i (Gomez 1998). European fascination for Hawaiian prints continues, as seen in Prada's 2003 menswear line inspired by Arthur's book *Aloha Attire* (Arthur 2000; Norwich 2003).

Discussion

The origins of the aloha shirt are multiethnic. European frock shirts and the Filipino *barong tagalog* provided the concept of a loose shirt worn outside the trousers; a closer fit, with collars and buttons, came from American businessmen. Japanese tailors provided kimono fabric and Chinese tailors did the bulk of custom tailoring in early twentieth-century Hawai'i. Textile designers came from a variety of ethnic backgrounds as well, and intentionally drew on the material culture of Asian and Pacific populations as they created textile designs. Consequently, the origins of the aloha shirt draw from four diverse ethnic groups; what they created was a garment that has come to represent the multiethnic population of Hawai'i.

Design motifs have continually been multiethnic as well, with definite trends occurring as particular events happened. For instance, prior to the Second World War, most of the designs were Japanese in origin. This is most probably a result of availability as the vast majority of the fabric in Hawai'i was then imported from Japan. However, politics became an issue. Once the war began, Japanese designs fell off significantly, as did

Chinese motifs. The ethnic population of Hawai'i had developed a symbolic affinity through the use of Hawaiian pidgin, and did much the same with the creation of a multiethnic garment, the aloha shirt. Dress as a form of material culture can provide a window through which we can examine culture; studies involving both primary and secondary sources, and both qualitative and quantitative methods, can provide for rich data.

This article posits that in a multiethnic society, such as Hawai'i, ethnic dress can function symbolically as a cultural marker representing the larger cultural value of embracing ethnic differences; in this case study then, ethnic dress represents inclusivity rather than exclusivity. The combination of pidgin and aloha shirts became symbolic of "local" identity, a form of pan-ethnic identity. By the 1960s "local" identity was well entrenched and at that time the aloha shirt followed two design paths, one for "locals" and the other for tourists and other outsiders. As a consequence, the aloha shirt proclaims a pan-ethnic identity and concurrently visually separates insiders and outsiders. For locals though, aloha attire is a visible manifestation of their multiethnic heritage. Lianne noted "It's about ethnic togetherness. When we have a family gathering, we wear aloha shirts and *mu'umu'u*. We aren't Japanese, Chinese or Filipinas— we're Hawaiian." Emphasizing the importance of regional ethnicity to local women, she went on to say, "It's *where* we are that makes us *who* we are."[20]

Notes

1. Aloha attire is a contemporary phrase referring to the Hawaiian-style garments made with tropical prints worn in Hawai'i today. Hawaiian dress has consistently avoided the use of waistlines, favoring a loose fit until recent times. The mainstay of the Hawaiian garment industry is the production of aloha shirts, *mu'umu'u* and *holomu'u*. *Holokū* are generally custom-made rather than commercially produced. Two of these garments were introduced in 1820 by Western missionaries— the *holokū*, originally a long loose dress with a train, but now Hawaii's formal gown, is often fitted, and the *mu'umu'u*, originally a chemise, is now a loose everyday dress. The *holomu'u* is a combination dress that is closely fitted, and long but without the train.
2. Most of the photos in this article are owned by the University of Hawaii CTAHR Historic Costume Collection, and were photographed by the author. Others are credited as appropriate.
3. Hawaii State Data Book. http://www.hawaii.gov/dbedt/db99/.
4. Hawai'i State Data Book. http://www.hawaii.gov/dbedt/db99/
5. Hawaiian Pidgin, from Wikipedia, the free encyclopedia. http://en.wikipedia.org/wiki/Hawaiian_pidgin.
6. Ibid.
7. DeSoto Brown and Gunter Von Hamm, interviews. Fall 1998.

8. Content analysis of design motifs found on 1930s aloha shirts showed that 44% had Japanese design motifs, while 12% were Chinese. By the end of the decade, Hawaiian motifs became quite popular and accounted for 23% of the motifs (see Table 1).

9. While a few rayon garments were produced in Hawai'i during this time period, the fabric was of inferior quality and did not hold color well. Virtually all the vintage garments still in existence made of Hawaiian prints on rayon were produced after the Second World War.

10. Sparkey Do. Interview, 9/98.

11. Content analysis of design motifs found on 1940s aloha shirts showed that 18% had Japanese design motifs, while 15% were Chinese. Hawaiian motifs accounted for 57% of the designs (see Table 1).

12. Alfred Shaheen, interview 2/1/99.

13. Alfred Shaheen, interview 2/1/99.

14. Of all the decades, the 1950s had the most Hawaiian design motifs in use, with fully 67% of the aloha shirts sporting Hawaiian designs. Nine percent were Japanese, 7% were Chinese, 7% were Polynesian, and 5% were Southeast Asian batiks (see Table 1).

15. DeSoto Brown, interview 6/6/99; Schiffer (1997: 38).

16. *Kapa* is the Hawaiian word for barkcloth, which was worn prior to the arrival of Westerners. Barkcloth in the rest of Polynesia is referred to as *tapa*.

17. Sales Builder, No. 7, Vol. 13. July 1940, p. 13.

18. Carol Pregill, President of Hawai'i Fashion Industry Association. Interview 1999.

19. In the 1970s, Hawaiian motifs accounted for 51% of the dominant motifs on aloha shirts while Polynesian and Hawaiian/Polynesian motifs accounted for 15% followed by 14% Japanese.

20. Lianne was a student at the University of Hawaii in 2000.

References

Anderson, Benedict. 1996. *Imagined Communities*. London: Verso.

Arien, Lorna. 1939. "Pins and Needles in Hawai'i: Honolulu's Newest Industry—Manufacturing Women's Clothes—Has Grown in the Last Two Years to Million Dollar Proportions." *The Honolulu Advertiser*, 2/19/39.

Arthur, Linda. 2000. *Aloha Attire: Hawaiian Dress in the Twentieth Century*. Atglen PA: Schiffer Publishing.

Barthes, Roland. 1983. *The Fashion System*. New York: Hill and Wang.

Bogatyrev, Petr. 1971. *The Functions of Folk Costume in Moravian Slovakia*. The Hague: Mouton.

Brown, DeSoto, and Linda Arthur. 2003. *The Art of the Aloha Shirt*. Honolulu: Island Heritage.

Buckridge, Steve. 2004. *Language of Dress: Resistance and Accommodation in Jamaica*

1750–1890. Kingston, Jamaica: University of West Indies Press.

Carrel, Barbara Goldman. 1999. "Hasidic Women's Head Coverings: A Feminized System of Hasidic Distinction." In Linda Arthur (ed.) Religion, Dress and the Body, pp. 163–99. Oxford: Berg.

Cheng, Susan, and T. Linh Ho. 2003. A Portrait of Race and Ethnicity in Hawaii. Honolulu: The Pacific American Research Center.

Cheng, Vincent. 2004. Inauthentic: The Anxiety over Culture and Identity. New Brunswick: Rutgers University Press.

Cohen, Abner. 1974. Urban Ethnicity. London: Tavistock.

Daly, Catherine M. 1999. "The Paarda Expression of Hejaab among Afghan Women in a Non-Muslim Community." In Linda Arthur (ed.) Religion, Dress and the Body, pp. 147–63. Oxford: Berg.

Dickson, Dee. 1979. "Hawaii, Fashions As Colorful as the Islands." Aloha Magazine.

Eicher, Joanne (ed.). 1995. Dress and Ethnicity. Oxford: Berg.

Eicher, Joanne, and Mary Ellen Roach Higgins. 1995. Dress and Identity. New York: Fairchild.

Funderburke, Emma. 1965. Garment Manufacturing Industry in Hawaii. Monograph. University of Hawaii Library.

Goffman, Erving. 1967. Interaction Ritual. New York: Doubleday.

Gomes, Andrew. 1998. "Uniforms Sustaining Life of Aloha Wear Manufacturers." Pacific Business News, 9/7/98.

Graybill, Beth, and Linda Arthur. 1999. "The Social Control of Women's Bodies in Two Mennonite Communities." In Linda Arthur (ed.) Religion, Dress and the Body, pp. 9–31. Oxford: Berg.

Green, Blake. 1985. "101 Uses For Aloha Attire." San Francisco Chronicle, 9/14/85: 13.

Haas, Michael. 1994. "Explaining Ethnic Harmony: Hawai'i's Multicultural Ethos." Paper presented at the American Sociological Association annual meeting, Los Angeles, CA.

Hope, Dale, and Gregory Tozian. 2000. The Aloha Shirt: Spirit of the Islands. Portland, OR: Beyond Words Publishing.

Irie, T. 1997. Master Book of Hawaiian Shirt. Tokyo: World Photo Press.

Jeffres, L.W. 2000. "Ethnicity and Ethnic Media Use." Communication Research 27(4): 496–535.

Kane, Herb Kawainui. 1986."The Shirt that Shouts Aloha!" Islands: 29–35.

Kirkpatrick, J. 1987. "Ethnic Antagonism and Innovation in Hawai'i." In J. Boucher, D. Landis, and K. Clark (eds) Ethnic Conflict: International Perspectives, pp. 298–316. Newbury Park: Sage.

Laroche M., C. Kim, M. Hui, and M. Tomiuk. 1998. "Test of a Nonlinear Relationship between Linguistic Acculturation and Ethnic Identification." Journal of Cross-Cultural Psychology 29(3): 418–33.

Laughlin, Barbara. n.d. Hawaiian Garment Companies. Unpublished manuscript.

Lenz, Carola. 1995. "Ethnic Conflict and Changing Dress Codes: A Case Study of an Indian Migrant Village in Highland Ecuador." In Joanne Eicher (ed.) Dress and Ethnicity, pp. 269–93. Oxford: Berg.

Lurie, Allison. 2000. The Language of Clothes. New York: Owl Books.

Lynch, Annette. 1995. "Hmong American New Year's Dress: The Display of Ethnicity." In Joanne Eicher (ed.) Dress and Ethnicity, pp. 255–67. Oxford: Berg.

McCracken, Grant. 1987. "Clothing as Language: An Object Lesson in the Study of the Expressive Properties of Material Culture." In Barrie Reynolds and Margaret Stott (eds) Material Anthropology: Contemporary Approaches to Material Culture, pp. 103–28. Lanham, MD: University Press of America.

Moor, Jonathan. 1978. "Hawaiian Punch." Gentlemen's Quarterly, Summer.

Nash, M. 1989. The Cauldron of Ethnicity in the Modern World. Chicago: University of Chicago Press.

Norwich, William. 2003. "A Shore Thing." Men's Fashions of the Times Magazine, March 9.

Phinney, Jean. 2005. "Ethnic Identity in Late Modern Times: A Response to Rattansi and Phoenix." Identity: An International Journal of Theory and Research 5(2): 187–94.

Okamura, Jon. 1984. "Why There are no Asian Americans in Hawai'i:

The Continuing Significance of Local Identity." *Social Process in Hawai'i* 35.

Rampell, Ed. 1999. "Hawaiiaan Manufacturers Find Gold Out West." *Pacific Business News* May 7.

Renee, Elisha. 2000. "Cloth and Conversion: Yoruba Textiles and Ecclesiastical Dress." In Linda Arthur (ed.) *Undressing Religion*, pp. 1–18. Oxford: Berg.

Schiffer, Nancy. 1997. *Hawaiian Shirt Designs*. Atglen, PA: Schiffer Publications.

Shirazi, Fagheh. 2000. "Islamic Religion and Women's Dress Code: The Islamic Republic of Iran." In Linda Arthur (ed.) *Undressing Religion*, pp. 103–33. Oxford: Berg.

Steele, Thomas. 1984. *The Hawaiian Shirt*. New York: Abbeville Press.

Stimpfl, Joseph. 2000. "Veiling and Unveiling: Reconstructing Malay Identity in Singapore." In Linda Arthur (ed.) *Undressing Religion*, pp. 166–80. Oxford: Berg.

Turner, Terrence. 1980. "The Social Skin." In Jeremy Cherfas and Roger Lewin (eds) *Not Work Alone: Cross-Cultural View of Activities Superfluous to Survival*, pp. 112–40. Beverly Hills, CA: Sage.

Waters, Mary. 1990. *Ethnic Options*. Berkeley: University of California Press.

Welters, Linda. 1995. "Ethnicity in Greek Dress." In Joanne Eicher (ed.) *Dress and Ethnicity*, pp. 53–77. Berg, Oxford.

Wentzel, Marty. 1989. "The Shirt that Says Aloha." *Pleasant Hawai'i*: 30–57.

Greek Sparto: Past and Present

Abstract

Sparto, a perennial broom, grows wild in the mountainous and semi-mountainous regions of the Mediterranean. Throughout antiquity Greeks processed the plant for its fibers, which they hand braided and loom wove into rope and textiles. Archaeological material and ancient testimonia demonstrate the extensive use of sparto as a raw material in Greek culture over a long period. Nevertheless, scholars consistently overlook the widespread exploitation of sparto in the manufacture of everyday objects in antiquity. However, the plant's importance may be properly assessed by modern Greeks. My field research in the Western Peloponesos reveals that the utilization and processing of sparto in recent times follows that described in ancient sources. The earliest archaeological evidence from sparto comes from a late, third-century (BC) Neolithic cave in Spain and includes various articles of clothing. The earliest Greek evidence comes from Homer who refers to ships' cords as "sparto" in the *Illiad*. Thereafter, a number of ancient authors mention sparto products that show close relationships to items made from the plant until recently. Moreover, Pliny's extended comments on sparto processing in the first century AD strikingly conform to the technical information supplied by modern Greeks.

HELEN BRADLEY FOSTER

Helen Bradley Foster received her Ph.D. from the Department of Folklore and Folklife at the University of Pennsylvania. She is an instructor in the Department of Art History, University of Minnesota. Foster conducts research in both the United States and Greece. Her publications on material culture include the books *New Raiments of Self: African American Clothing in the Antebellum South* (1997) and *Wedding Dress Across Cultures* (2003), co-edited with Donald Clay Johnson.

Textile, Volume 4, Issue 1, pp. 36–67
Reprints available directly from the Publishers.
Photocopying permitted by licence only.
© 2006 Berg. Printed in the United Kingdom.

Greek Sparto: Past and Present

Sparto, a perennial broom, grows wild over much of the Mediterranean region in brushwood localities of the mountain and semi-mountain zones which include the western Peloponnesos, the area of Greece under study.[1] *Gray's Manual of Botany* places sparto as a member of the *Gramineae*, or Grass, family (*Spartium junceum L.*).[2] Its common English name is Spanish Broom (Figure 1). The shrub, not reaching over 3 m in height, has small leaves usually absent except during wet springs. Its abundant green branches are slender and sharply pointed. Small, bright-yellow flowers, 2.5 cm across, form spikes at the ends of stems and appear from May through July (Sfikas 1978: 26; for the varieties of wild Greek broom plants, see Sfikas 1990: 96–101; Spanish Broom, pp. 100-101).

Contemporary Greek women preserve a folk custom associated with flowering sparto that may be compared to other European customs involving this plant. On the first of May, Greek women weave flowering sparto branches into wreaths and hang them above doorways. This May Day tradition, and the particular use of yellow flowers, appears to be widespread over the continent. Larch S. Garrad reports that on May Eve, on the Isle of Man "as elsewhere in Europe, yellow blooms of green branches were used to decorate and protect the house ..." (1984: 76). Particular favorites there were primroses and marsh marigolds.

In the nineteenth century, Thiselton Dyer noted this bit of lore: "the broom having plenty of blossoms is a sign of a fruitful year" (1889: 117). This belief perhaps accounts for the Greek custom of fashioning blossoming sparto branches into May wreaths for their homes. But J.D.A. Widdowson notes a contrary belief in some parts of Great Britain where "there is a strong resistance to the bringing of broom flowers into the house during the month of May." He records an old rhyme: "He who brings broom into the house in May/Sweeps the head of the house away" (1984: 226–7). A hundred years earlier, Dyer offered this variant from Sussex in the south of England: "If you sweep the house with blossomed broom in May/You are sure to sweep the head of the house away" (1889: 274).

Dyer also remarked on an herbal amulet which included broom: "nowadays, when [rue is] worn on the person in conjunction with agrimony, maiden-hair, broom-straw, and ground ivy, it is said in the Tyrol to confer fine vision, and to point out the presence of witches" (1889: 56).

I elicited no such medical or supernatural beliefs about sparto from modern Greeks. Except for May wreaths, they apparently do not attach any cosmological importance to the plant. Rather, the Greeks follow their ancient forebears and associate sparto with uses of a more ordinary nature.

Figure 1
Wild sparto in bloom.

For at least 2,000 years, rural Greeks gathered sparto to manufacture rope and textiles. Information recently supplied to me by modern Greek contributors and the evidence found in ancient testimonia support this claim. In spite of its lengthy use, however, there is only rare textual information about sparto for the period between the first century A.D. and the present. The lack of documentation through the Greek War of Independence (1821–35) is accountable to the fact that, because foreign overlords ruled Greece during the intervening centuries, written records about the daily lives of ordinary people remain largely untranslated if, indeed, they ever existed. More difficult to understand is the nearly non-existent textual information on sparto since Greek independence. Among the few modern, popular references to sparto as a plant fiber that I have located in Greece are a brief entry on processing "broom" in *Catalogue* to the collection, Peloponnesian Folklore

Foundation (1981: 9), and an even briefer note in the Museum of Greek Folk Art's pamphlet guide stating that "broom" is one of the "raw materials used in weaving ..." (n.d., n.p.n). In this article I attempt to correct the omission of sparto from the literature on contemporary Greek handmade textile production. My second aim is to use the modern information on the plant as a means of hypothesizing about its exploitation in the everyday lives of ancient Greeks.

Lack of documentation may be accounted for in several ways. The reasons relate to the gender-orientations of earlier and more recent ethnographers, as well as to the timing of the later ethnographers' arrival. According to the age of my contributors, and the fact that they learned about sparto from their mothers and grandmothers, the plant was being used in the late nineteenth century when the first ethnographies of rural Greek communities began. These early reports, however, contain no mention of the customs surrounding sparto, although cursory observations are made of women involved in tasks associated with the manufacture of textiles from other fibers. The reason for only circumstantial references to women in turn-of-the-century ethnographers' reports is understandable: the earliest folklorists and anthropologists working among rural Greeks were men who focused on male activities, and who noted household chores only in passing. As Warren Roberts writes concerning his own fieldwork today: "Certain things

are thought to be men's work and certain things are thought to be women's work, and men have only a superficial knowledge about and very little interest in women's work ..." (1988: 23).

Roberts' comment is well illustrated in the following two passages. Rennell Rodd's cryptic observation in 1892 is an early ethnographic note on fabric production in Greece: "All the women who have not gone out to the fields to work with the men will be spinning in the doorways or weaving at the loom ..." (1892: 57). About two decades later, an equally oblique statement comes from Alan Wace and Maurice Thompson who mention that, "For the greater part of the day we shall find the housewife in the work-room at her spinning wheel, an elder daughter will be at the loom ..." (1914: 95).

Once women ethnographers went into the field, women became important subjects of study with the result that their daily lives became a matter of record. Nevertheless, ethnographic reports by women scholars, who otherwise fully detail women's work, do not mention sparto (cf. Clark 1976; Dubisch 1986; DuBoulay 1974; Friedl 1962; Koster 1976). In a similar manner, Greek weaver, Anna Sikeltanos, mentions "utilizing materials offered by the environment—wool, cotton, flax, silk, or even hemp" on her loom, but makes no mention of sparto (1988: 124).

Two possibilities may explain these more recent omissions by women scholars. First, it may be that in the particular field-study regions in which they worked, sparto simply was not gathered and woven. Second, it may be that by the mid-1950s, when Ernestine Friedl conducted the first modern ethnographic study in Greece in which extensive details about women's roles were included, the custom of weaving sparto had already disappeared. This supposition arises from my interviews with modern Greeks.

Although one elderly woman reported to me that she processed sparto and wove with it until twenty years ago, most of the women I interviewed said that they stopped using sparto fiber about forty or fifty years ago. That is, from the early 1950s onwards when inexpensive, commercially produced fabrics and clothing became readily obtainable, and caused a decline in some traditions associated with handmade textile manufacture such as the processing and spinning of natural plant fibers to be woven.

Modern Greeks fill in the missing documentation on this once widely used, and extremely serviceable plant. I first describe the fieldwork region and the modern contributors to this study. The main portion of the text is devoted to the recollections of older, rural Greeks concerning gathering, processing and weaving. To demonstrate the timeless nature of the methods involved in processing sparto, whenever possible, the modern information will be prefaced with comparable information from Pliny the Elder, who wrote in the first century AD.[3] Sparto is then contextualized within individual and communal lifestyles. The conclusion explores reasons for the demise of

sparto's use as a textile plant in Greece.

I provide two Appendices. The first annotates passages from Pliny and other ancient sources which pertain to the exploitation of sparto in antiquity as well as archaeological evidence for the plant's use. Appendix II lists modern Greek places that take their names from the root word "sparto."

Fieldwork Region and Contributors: Recollections and Demonstrations

Information about sparto was collected during the summers of 1990 and 1991 from male and female inhabitants of four, small agrarian villages in the province *nomos* Eleias on the west coast of the Peloponnesos. Two of the villages, Neohorio and Kakovatos, are situated in a plain along the Ionian Sea. The inhabitants of Neohorio and Kakovatos descend from settlers who came from villages in the foothills of Arkadia. Villagers from two of these older hill villages, Krisahori and Kalidona, were also interviewed.

Evagelika (born 1944) is a primary contributor who volunteered to demonstrate the step-by-step procedures for processing sparto. This occurred on two days in mid-August 1991, and is referred to as "the demonstration." From gathering sparto to weaving its fibers into a product, the basic steps include:

1. gathering—cutting branches; trimming the soft, pliable branches from the harder stalk; tying the branches into bundles;

2. boiling and soaking the bundles in water;
3. beating the outer husk;
4. extracting the fibers;
5. cleaning and combing the fibers;
6. spinning the fibers into thread;
7. weaving or braiding the thread.

Concerning these steps, recollections from all Greek contributors were quite similar; variations in procedures indicate customs particular to a specific village or within an individual family.

Gathering
The steps demonstrated by modern women closely parallel Pliny's valuable and succinctly descriptive passages from the first century BC: "Esparto is also a plant, which is self-sown and cannot be grown from seed; strictly it is a rush, belonging to a dry soil ... it is [gathered] ... most easily between the middle of May to the middle of June, which is the season when the plant ripens" (19.26.7).

Ikatina (1910(?)–98) said that her family gathered sparto in late spring or early summer; Tasia (born 1929) said her family gathered it in September. Yiannis (born 1912), who showed us sparto growing wild in Kalidona in mid-July, indicated that the sparto was ready to cut at that time. Evagelika reported that sparto can be collected from the end of June to the beginning of August, but the sparto she cut for the demonstration was actually gathered in mid-August. More specifically, Evagelika explained that the branches must not have tough husks at their ends.

What is evident from these statements is that sparto must be gathered in the summer months after the inner fibers mature, but before the plant becomes dormant. Evagelika summed it up with an idiomatic expression: "The sparto must be *psemena*." *Psemena* literally refers to perfectly roasted beef; in this sense it means the sparto must be "just right": not too soft, not too hard.

Ikatina mentioned that her entire family gathered the sparto, and Tasia said that men helped to cut and haul it. On the other hand, Evagelika stated that only women cut it, and that it had to be cut correctly. She and her sister, as the oldest of ten children, were given this job. Evagelika remembered: "For the preparing of sparto, I used to help from eight years old until 1956, when I left my village in order to study."

Sparto was never cultivated, and so all contributors told of gathering sparto from the wild. Ikatina remembers that when she was a girl, her entire family left their home village, Taxiarchi, and went to Kalidona to gather the sparto which grew in the area. Food and pack animals were taken and her family stayed with relatives in Kalidona. After the sparto was cut and bundled, it was packed onto the animals and taken back to Taxiarchi for processing. Yiannis, who showed us the sparto growing wild on a hillside in his village, said that it was gathered from this source. Evagelika gathered the sparto she used for the demonstration from along the shoulders of the national highway.[4]

Soaking

Pliny: "the plant being soaked for ten days [in 'Asia']" (19.15).

The first day of Evagelika's demonstration concerned the soaking procedure. Besides Evagelika, the people gathered included two of Evagelika's sons, Evagelika's next-door neighbor, Kaliopi (born 1917), a teenage male visiting Angelika from Athens, several of Evagelika's teenage neighbors (male and female), Gigi Cooper (my American interpreter), Jamie Cole (an American friend), and myself.

Before the fibers can be extracted, the cut and trimmed sparto branches must be soaked in water to soften them in preparation for stripping the outer fibers from the woody stems. This process, known as retting, is used to soften other bast fibers such as flax and hemp. Most contributors related that this step first entailed making bundles of sparto branches which were then placed in a stream of cold, running water for ten days. Rocks laid on the bundles kept them weighted down in the water.[5]

Evagelika also described soaking sparto in running water, but she explained that, in addition, her family boiled the sparto branches before soaking them for five to seven days.[6] Evagelika carried out an abbreviated version of the boiling procedure by placing four previously cut and neatly trimmed bundles of sparto in a large pot of boiling water over a single-burner camp stove in her kitchen (Figure 2). Under more ordinary circumstances, boiling adds an arduous task to the process because, in order to do this, a large cauldron of water must

Figure 2
Evagelika boils the sparto in her kitchen.

be set up outside and brought to boil by open fire.[7] As the sparto boiled, it gave off an odor that continued to be omitted during the entire period of soaking. The Greek euphemism for sparto during this stage is *merisa*: "it stinks."

Evagelika allowed the sparto to boil for about one hour. Then, to test if it peeled easily, she ran a fingernail down the outer skin of a stem. She then removed the sparto bundles from the hot water and took them outside to her backyard where she placed them in a large, plastic garbage can filled with hose water. During the seven days in which the bundles soaked, the water was changed twice daily.

Beating

Pliny: "After that it is pounded to make it serviceable" (19.26.8).

Seven days after the initial demonstration at Evagelika's,

Gigi, Jamie, and I returned to watch the next procedures. Again, about fifteen family members and neighbors of all ages and both sexes were on hand.

When the soaking period has elapsed, the first task involves removing the sparto bundles from the water and then pounding them, which breaks the outer husk to facilitate extraction of the inner fibers. During the course of this project, Evagelika wrote her recollections of the traditions and processes concerning the use of sparto among rural Greeks (August 15, 1990).[8]

Evagelika began this part of the demonstration by taking a fistful of bundled stems from the water and placing them on a flat rock. These she beat with a wooden paddle (Figure 3). She occasionally dipped the bundles back into the pail of water. On the final beating, she

said that one must get out as much water as possible.

During my fieldwork, I showed several contributors a wooden tool (Figure 4), and all said it was used to break sparto. Nonetheless, no one had such a tool.[9] Instead, they indicated various other implements which they used to beat the stems. Evagelika's pounding tool was a broken, short-handled wooden paddle, formerly used for washing clothes. Tasia beat sparto stems with a flat, short-handled wooden *plasteri*, a tool usually used to handle bread loaves in an outdoor bake oven.

Extracting the Fibers

Stripping entails removing the softened fibers from the beaten stems (Figure 5). Amy Kakissis' uncle said that it takes one person five days to strip the fiber from 100 lbs of sparto (June 1991). During

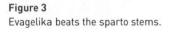

Figure 3
Evagelika beats the sparto stems.

Evagelika's demonstration, the fibers were easily extracted even though the branches had been soaked for a shorter period than the ten days which others said was necessary. Thus, Evagelika's method of parboiling, which softens the stems, allows the cold-water soaking time to be cut.

The woody stems which remain after stripping serve a variety of purposes. They are saved to be used as kindling for fires (Figure 6).

Pliny: "country people use it for ... fuel and torches" (19.26.8).

Or, they may be made into serviceable products. Evagelika, for example, bundled a bunch of

Figure 4
Handmade wooden implement, used to break flax or sparto, found abandoned in region of fieldwork.

Figure 5
Kaliopi stripping fibers from the beaten sparto.

Figure 6
After stripping, sparto stems are used as fire kindling.

stems and tied them to make a whisk broom (Figure 7). She also said that the stems may be woven into baskets.

Cleaning and Combing

As the fibers are pulled from the stems, they are spread out in the sun to dry. Once dried, they are gathered up for the next process—that of cleaning and combing. The course balls of extracted fiber are knotted and contain bits of stem and, therefore, must be refined before they can be spun (Figure 8). To aid in this task, Greek women employ heckles (also utilized to clean wool and flax; Figure 9). Heckles are a pair of short-handled, paddle-shaped wooden boards into which metal teeth are inserted.[10] Tasia and Evagelika each retain their handmade heckles and individually they demonstrated how to use them to clean the fibers of chaff and to untangle and make them soft.

The method for combing sparto proceeds in the following manner. A ball of fibers is loosely woven into the teeth of one heckle which is held stationary. The other heckle is then combed through the fibers. As these fibers are pulled out, they are repacked into the teeth of the first heckle and recombed.

Because this process is time-consuming, it is often put off until the winter months. Evagelika remembers this about the combing process during her childhood: "All the family members clean it. This happens during the long winter nights around the fireplace. The fibers are combed and rolled into balls ... Afterwards, the grandmother, if available, and the mother spin the fibers and it comes out as thread."

Spinning

Clearly a time-consuming task, Amy Kakissis' uncle told her that it takes one person four to five days to drop spin 100 lbs of sparto fiber (June 1991). In Greece, upright spinning wheels with foot treadles are rare. The two mechanisms usually employed for spinning are a low, vertical hand wheel or a

Figure 7
Striped sparto stems made into a
whisk broom.

drop spindle. Most Greek women who spin are able to operate either type. A village *mastoras* (master craftsman) made Tasia's *anamithi* (spinning wheel) sometime after 1942 (Figure 10). She employed it only to spin wool, not sparto. This type of spinning wheel has another separate part, the *anemi*, the rack around which the spun thread is held.

In several ways, the simpler drop spindle (Figure 11) is more practical than a spinning wheel. Unlike a wheel, a drop spindle is easily portable, and Greek women often employed it when away from home watching grazing goat and sheep flocks. The manufacture of a drop spindle is less complicated than the building of a spinning wheel. There are two parts to a drop spindle. One part, the distaff (*roka*), holds the ball of combed fibers to be spun. Intricately carved wooden distaffs form collections in all Greek folk museums; yet, as was demonstrated on several occasions during this study, a simple, forked stick serves just as well as a carved distaff. For instance, when asked about spinning one day, Tasia merely picked a forked stick from her wood pile and proceeded to tie a ball of sparto fibers into the fork as a prelude to spinning. Likewise, when I asked about spinning during the demonstration at Evagelika's home, Kaliopi picked

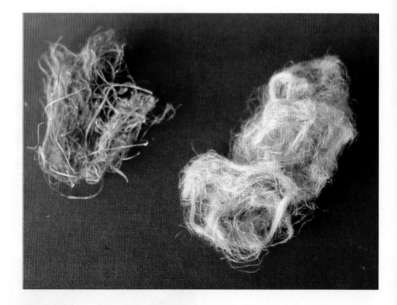

Figure 8
Sparto fibers before and after combing.

Figure 9
Evagelika's handmade heckles.

up a stick from the yard and broke it to form a fork at one end. A ball of fibers was then tied into the notch of this stick (Figure 12).

The other part of the drop spindle is the drop itself. The drop is simply a shaft, weighted at the bottom with a whorl. The shaft used on the day of the demonstration was an ordinary, machine-milled wooden dowel without a whorl. And, when someone else wanted to spin, a piece of dry bamboo picked up from the yard became a shaft. Occasionally the whorl is decorated with carving, but never with the intricacy of the distaff. Further

Figure 10
Tasia's handmade spinning wheel (*anamithi*) and separate handmade rack (*anemi*), which holds spun threads.

evidence of the makeshift tools which might be employed in drop spinning occurred when Evagelika poked a raw onion onto the bottom of the stick to serve as a whorl.

Spinning with a drop spindle takes practice and dexterity. First, a ball of combed fibers is tied into the notch of the distaff. The long handle of the distaff is then tucked firmly under the arm of the person who will spin and its bottom end is tied to the person's waist, leaving both hands free to control the fibers. Spinning proceeds as the drop is kept turning and fibers are continuously pulled from the distaff and twisted around the drop stick. This process creates a strong, unbroken strand of thread. Yet even when spinning with improvised tools, the Greek women I watched were adept at transforming the sparto fibers into a tightly twisted, smooth thread.

Weaving

Pliny: "Country people there [the Cartagena section of Hither Spain] use it for ... footwear and for shepherd's clothes" (19.26.7); "one who wishes to understand the value of this marvelous plant must realize how much it is employed in all countries for the rigging of ships, for mechanical appliances used in building, and for other requirements of life" (19.26.7).

Once enough thread has been spun, it is ready to be either hand-braided or loom-woven into a product. In modern times, women wove sparto to produce several items. Evagelika mentioned that sparto was hand-braided to make ropes to tie up animals. She showed two ways to braid rope from sparto fibers. A finer rope is produced by braiding three strands. A heavier rope is produced by braiding five strands, each of which has been previously braided from four strands.

Evagelika also noted that sparto fibers were used to fill comforters, and she recalled another use for the plant: "After the German occupation of 1940, when Greece fell into poverty, they used to make slippers [of sparto]; for the sole they used the skin of pigs [made] especially soft by processing that in water. Women and children used to wear mostly these slippers, and the life of the slippers was about fifteen to thirty days."[11]

In 1991, Anthony Aphouros' Macedonian grandmother (age eighty-nine) described to her grandchildren the processing of sparto. Anthony reports that in that region of Greece, "They made everything from sparto." When questioned, he said that undergarments were not woven from sparto because the fabric

Figure 11
Evagelika using an improvised drop spindle. Note onion employed as a spindle whorl.

was too rough; but he noted that besides ropes, carpets and bed covers, they made a cape or cloak of woven sparto to be worn in winter "like Mexicans wear."[12]

Contributors from the western Peloponnesos, however, reported that sparto was loom-woven into carpets, and bedspreads (Figures 13 and 14), but that it was never used to make clothing. Ikatina and Tasia were both especially emphatic in this regard. And when Evagelika's son, Stomatos, remarked that only poor people wove with sparto, the rich used wool, Evagelika amended by saying that, in the past, everyone used sparto to make carpets. Of loom-woven items, Evagelika

Figure 12
Distaff (*roka*) made from a forked
stick holds sparto fibers for spinning.

Figure 13
Hard-loomed carpets airing, Samikon,
1995.

Figure 14
Tasia's sparto bedspread, woven
before 1942.

summarized: "sparto thread is useful for weaving ruglets, coverlets, sacks, and other useful items for the family."[13]

Performance: Past and Present, Individual and Communal

The processing of sparto entailed gender-specific jobs. This division of labor, however, might differ within individual families. Usually men made the more refined spinning and weaving tools and, in the past, men carved distaffs with elaborate designs as gifts for future brides. The Greek women who retain the tools associated with producing textiles often mention the men who made them. Tasia said that her neighbor, Paniotis, made her *plasteri* and *anamithi*, and that her father made her *anemi*. Evagelika combed the sparto fibers with the heckles which she said her father-in-law crafted.[14] Besides constructing tools, in some families men and young boys also helped in the early stages of gathering and preparing the sparto fibers. Evagelika said that in her village, the only jobs which males performed were stripping the fibers and, later, cleaning them: "Boys had different work to do." Women always performed the final tasks of spinning and weaving no matter the fiber. The end products, whether clothing made from cotton and flax, or rope, bed coverlets, and carpets made from sparto, were used by all family members.

Older Greeks are aware that machine-manufactured textiles and other commercially produced objects are replacing items which they once manufactured at home. Men, as well as women, willingly contributed to this study by telling what they knew about processing sparto. They take pride in sharing their knowledge of the craft as shown, for instance, by Yiannis and Yorgios who located and cut sparto for us, and as exhibited by the women who assisted in numerous ways with this project.

In particular, Evagelika's stated reasons for helping me best exemplify this concern for maintaining knowledge of past traditions. Evagelika is an elementary-school teacher who demonstrates for her young students the techniques involved in producing archaic rural Greek handicrafts because, she says, "They don't know anything about these things." Although sparto was gathered, processed, and woven during Evagelika's childhood, she relates that when she left her village she did not continue the tradition; thus, her four sons (born 1966, 1969, 1970, and 1974) were unaware of sparto's use for textiles until she offered to show me about it. Evagelika further showed her eagerness to pass on the custom by giving me entries from Greek encyclopedias on both linen and sparto and by writing out the entire sparto process as she remembered it from her childhood, illustrating her text with drawings (Figure 15). By testifying to the use of sparto, the older people continue to pass on the tradition and thereby keep its memory alive.

Many women currently purchase mass-produced textile items; they nonetheless retain the tools associated with making cloth. For instance, Kaliopi wove her last rug about fifteen years ago, after which she took apart her loom and stored it in an outbuilding. In August 1991, however, she removed the loom from storage for the first time in more than a decade in order to demonstrate weaving. Tasia has not woven for a number of years and, in a similar manner, the loom which she formerly set up in the yard in warm weather, or in her home in the winter, was taken apart and is now stored in a shed. But, like Kaliopi, Tasia also brought out her loom for the first time in several years for the purpose of showing it to me. During interviews, Kaliopi, Tasia, and Evagelika each eagerly retrieved from storage other textile-related tools and demonstrated their use. Thus, the heckles, spinning wheels, and looms now function as heirlooms; and an important purpose for keeping these tools is to share with others knowledge of the crafts which in the past occupied so much of a rural woman's lifetime.[15]

Women also retain their handmade textiles and are equally willing to display them. For instance, during the past fifteen years I have visited Tasia many times at her home where she always invited me into her kitchen, but never into the more private family quarters. The only time that Tasia invited me into that section of her house was to show me the carpets she had prepared for her daughter's dowry. Kaliopi, too, showed the rag rugs that she wove, as did Ikatina (Figure 16). And Evagelika not only exhibited a very long sparto rug, hand-dyed and woven by her mother, but she also insisted on cutting off a section as a gift to me (Figure 17).

In the past, procedures associated with the refining of sparto took on a communal outlook. Evagelika highlights this comradery with her remarks about women joining together when the sparto stems were beaten.

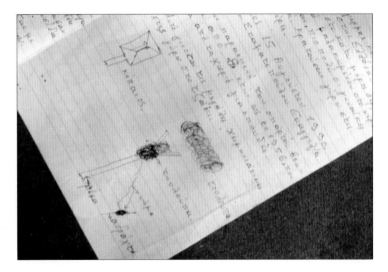

Figure 15
Evagelika's written and illustrated instructions for processing sparto.

Figure 16
Ikatina's sparto rug.

Though spinning is done by a single person, this task often takes place in a social gathering. Kaliopi says that women gathered in each other's homes to clean and to spin sparto. She explains that first they would get together in one home, then in another. The spinning session at Evagelika's certainly proved to be a social occasion for the older women who were present. Each took turns showing their skill at spinning; and when they attempted to instruct me in the technique of drop spinning, they thereby were embracing another woman into their company (Figure 18).

Figure 17
A remnant of Evagelika's sparto rug.

Figure 18
The expert spinners instruct me.

Sparto processing was resurrected as a communal event during the two sessions at Evagelika's house when neighbors and family members gathered to act as both participants and as audience for the demonstration. Besides the roles played by older women, two other performance patterns emerged. First are the roles obviously marked by the sex of the individuals. For example, two of Evagelika's sons acted as interpreters, and one prepared the garbage can by filling it with water. The latter son also entertained the group by giving a solo performance of male Cretan dances at the end of the first day's work (Figure 19). On the other hand, only the older women performed the tasks of beating, stripping, refining, and spinning.[16]

The second role pattern which emerged has to do with age. As with many crafts in the past, those associated with handmade textiles

Figure 19
Stomatos entertains with Cretan dances.

were learned informally. All women interviewed said they had learned to spin and weave from an older female relative. With the decline in home-manufacture of fabric, these techniques are not being passed on. This example of recent alterations in rural Greek society was strikingly confirmed during the demonstration. During the two days, not one of the younger Greek women joined in to help with any of the tasks; whereas, in the near past, these younger women would have been expected to learn by doing in order to carry on the age-old traditions (Figure 20). This modern definition of women's roles goes a long way toward explaining the loss of customs surrounding sparto.

"Now We Can Buy Everything"
In Greece, textiles are second only to the combined production of food, beverages, and tobacco in gross domestic manufacture. Cotton and cotton by-products are the number one textile. Jute, flax, and hemp are still grown commercially in Greece, but to a lesser extent than cotton. Thus, several plants known for their properties in manufacturing textiles remain under cultivation. Sparto, a non-cash crop, once also commonly used in rural communities, has been abandoned. What factors account for its demise in popularity? Most obvious is that, aside from the ancient use of sparto in the manufacture of ship's rope, the custom of processing the plant into useful items has been practiced only among rural folk, the end-product being used only within the immediate community.

As in the Balkans generally, the Industrial Revolution affected Greece later than it did other, more technically advanced Western nations. Nevertheless, recent changes associated with textile manufacture in Greece have brought about a swift decline in the home production of fabrics. The decline is dated to the early 1950s when commercially produced textiles became readily available

Figure 20
Young women observed, but did not participate.

and affordable. Because it is no longer necessary to perform the arduous and time-consuming labor involved in producing woven items, the tasks of gathering, cleaning, and spinning plant or animal fibers have been abandoned by all but a few older women.

In the last four decades, lifestyles traditionally associated with self-sufficient agrarian families have been undergoing changes in Greece: children—girls as well as boys—now attend schools of higher education in preparation for jobs not associated with the land; immigration to other countries and migration to Greek urban centers accelerates; and newer technologies, such as telephones, televisions, computers, and motorized farm vehicles, are being adopted. New lifestyles mean that many familial tasks which once had to be performed have undergone modification or have been abandoned altogether.

Though contributors commented specifically about sparto, their remarks are relevant to views held about other hand-gathered fibers as well. Commercially produced fabrics gained favor as a sign of prosperity and are qualified as more favorable than those produced at home. Yiannis reported that the women in his village stopped gathering sparto in the 1950s because "now there are many more different kinds of cloth which may be purchased," demonstrating with his hands how fabric is unrolled from huge bolts in stores. Ikatina said she stopped gathering sparto because the textile items "sold in stores are more beautiful than hand-woven items." Tasia explained that most women stopped gathering sparto after the Greek Civil War (which ended in 1950) because, "Now, we can buy everything."

Domestic loom weaving, itself, continues as a craft among some older women. Yet even this tradition altered once ready-made fabrics became inexpensively available. For instance, the items still most commonly hand-woven are carpets; but now, rather than first producing the threads to be woven for these carpets, machine-made rags are used. Kaliopi wove her last carpets out of machine-made rags, and the pile of about twenty rag carpets that Tasia wove as part of her daughter's dowry were all made from commercially produced fabric.[17]

As we sat and talked after the conclusion of the final demonstration, Evagelika remarked that when she and Kaliopi were young they were very poor, and because of this, family members were expected to be proficient in a number of handicrafts in order to insure the survival of all. The worldwide depression in the 1930s, followed by the German occupation during the Second World War, immediately followed by the Greek Civil War (1948–50) caused the poverty which Evagelika, Kaliopi, and many Greeks experienced. Now, the generation which knew terrible crises of privation eagerly embraces modern conveniences, as do their children. The adoption of commercially produced textiles is evidence of this grasp toward modernity. The specific abandonment of sparto as a textile plant represents but a single aspect of the general trend away from the use of many hand-manufactured items, but it serves as an indicator of broader dynamics within contemporary Greek society (Figure 21).

Appendix 1: Annotated Ancient Testimonia and Archaeological Evidence

Classical Sources: Pliny's Contribution

Pliny suggests that sparto is indigenous to Greece, and that although in Roman times the supply came from the northern Mediterranean—Africa and especially from Spain—the Carthaginians ultimately imported the plant from Greece. Archaeological evidence from Spain, however, pre-dates material remains or any textual references from Greece. Elizabeth J.W. Barber discusses the oldest known objects fashioned from sparto fibers. These objects, found in a Spanish cave and dated to the late third millennium BC, include: "baskets, sandals, bags, caps, and even full tunics and a necklace" (1991: 32–3). Using this and other evidence, Barber then argues that sparto "was essentially unused outside its native regions of southern Spain and northern Africa before the export trade of Classical times" (1991: 34); that is, not until the fifth century BC.

Regarding Bronze-Age Greece, Barber says, "silk, cotton, and esparto, although used elsewhere in quantity at the time, were surely not available here" (1991: 35). The latter premise is debatable, however; for, if Pliny's interpretation that Homer's use of the word "sparto" for rope means that the rope was made from the plant of that name, then this pre-dates the existence of either Spain or Africa as named places, and indicates that the Greeks were using sparto at least by the time of the earliest recorded Greek history, well before the Classical period.

On Rope

Ancient and modern Greeks referred to the plant as "sparto," which translates into the English "broom." The botanical classification for sparto (commonly, Spanish Broom) is *Spartium junceum L.*, Grass family. Both genus and species terms, *Spartium* and *junceum*, are associated with words for "rope." *Spartium* comes "from the Greek *spartine*, 'a cord,' such as was made from the bark of *Spartium* or broom" (*Gray's Manual of Botany* 1950: 179). The English word "junk", from *junceum*, originally meant old rope (*Webster's Third New International* 1961). Strabo (born first century BC) gives an etymological deduction for *junceum* when he describes the inhabitants of the island of Corcyra: "The Emporitans are quite skillful in flax-working. As for the inland territory which they hold, one part of it is fertile, while the other produces the spart [*sic*] of the rather useless, or rush, variety; it is called 'Juncarian' Plain" (3.4.9). Strabo continues, but this time he uses the popular name of the plant to name the region: "[The road]

Figure 21
Machine-made rugs for sale, Athens, 1994.

gradually departs what is called the Spartian—or, as we should say, 'Rush'—Plain. This plain is large and has no water, but produces the kind of spart [*sic*] that is suitable for twisting ropes, and is therefore exported to all regions, and particularly to Italy" (3.4.9).

So closely was the plant associated with rope making that the ancient Greeks used the word "sparto" synonymously to mean "rope" or "cord." For example, the following translation of Herodotus (fifth century BC) reads: "They make a cord [*sparto*] fast to the feet of their little children, lest the children fall into the water" (V.16). From the same century, Thucydides writes that the Corcyraeans strangled "themselves with the cords [*spartois*] from some beds that happened to be in the place..." (4.48.3). Aristotle (fourth century BC) uses the term *sparton* to mean "cord" or "rope" in describing the methods used to solve several mechanical problems (e.g., *Mechanical*

Problems 1–2, 849b; 3, 850a; 20–21, 853b, 854a).

Pliny indirectly refers to sparto as a material for making rope when he relates that "sluggard," a member of Socrates' group, was "represented [iconographically] as twisting a rope of broom which an ass is nibbling" (35.40.138). The commentator notes: "Hence a Latin proverb: *ocnus spartum torquens*, 'sloth twisting a rope'" (Pliny 1952: 360–61). From the same period, Xenophon describes the traps set for deer in the mountains, and here the "cord" is definitely made from sparto: "The noose of the cord to be laid on the crown and the cord itself should be of woven *sparto*, since this is rot-proof" (9.13).

In particular, a number of early historical references firmly support sparto's use in the production of ship's rope. Pliny writes: "King Antichos would only allow ropes made from this Syrian papyrus to be used in his navy, the employment of esparto not yet having become general"

(13.24.73). J.S. Morrison and J.F. Coates interpret Athenaeus (first century BC):

In the third century BC materials for the ropes made for a ship built for Hiero of Syracuse consisted of leukia, a variety of esparto grass, and hemp (Kannabis) and pitch from Rhôdes (Athenaeus 5.40.206). These fibers were presumably more readily available in Syracuse than flax and papyrus which were the alternative materials for ropes, as they were for sails in the eastern Mediterranean. (1987: 191)

Other Uses

While the ancient sources refer to rope as the product most often made from sparto, the plant clearly was being used in antiquity for a variety of other purposes and to produce a number of other products. For example, Dioscorides (first century AD) gives the medicinal properties for sparto seeds, flowers, and stems (4.158; 1968: 552–3). Pliny, meanwhile, tells that the plant's flowers were a source of nectar: "It is a mistake to say that esparto grass is also an exception, because a great deal of the honey obtained in the broom thickets of Spain tastes of that plant" (9.8.18).

Pliny noted that the rural people of Cartegena Spain made footwear and shepherd's clothes from sparto. Much earlier evidence for the ancient production of clothing fabric from sparto in Greece comes from Plato (427–347 BC), who mentions the "manufacture of cloth made from flax [*linon*] and broom-cord [*sparton*]" (280C.).

Linen, Sparto, and Linear B: Toward a Folk Taxonomy

While ancient sources supply ample testimonia about sparto, they provide many more references to flax, whose end-product is linen.[18] Both plants produce bast fibers and, therefore, are processed in nearly the same way. Sparto, however, produces courser fibers than does flax. Furthermore, although wild flax does grow in Greece, most is harvested from domestically grown crops whereas sparto is always gathered from the wild.

Pliny the Elder comments often on flax, and not only for its properties in the manufacture of linen. For instance, he writes that "the thistle-finch weaves its nest out of flax..." (10.49.96); and he reports on the positive effects of using linseed oil as medicine (e.g. 20.92.249 and 28.16.62).

Pausanias (second century AD) mentions flax used for textiles. Of

significance, these entries from Pausanias concern the region of *Eleia/Elis*, which is the modern province of *Eleias*, the area of my fieldwork. "[T]he surprising natural features of Eleia are firstly the linen flax which grows only here and nowhere else in Greece, and secondly the fact that Elean mares are impregnated by donkeys outside the territory of Elis, but not inside it ... For its fineness Elean linen flax is just as good as Jewish, though not so tawny" (5.5.2).

In another passage Pausanias continues to record his knowledge of the Elean cultivation of textile plants: "The Elean territory is productive and fruitful and among other crops particularly good for fine flax. People whose soil is right for it sow hemp and flax and fine flax ..." (6.6).

Pausanias mentions "sowing," thus making it certain that he was referring to cultivated flax and not to wild sparto. While doing this research, however, I often found that modern Greeks make a less-clear distinction between the two plants. Literally, *linaria* is *linum* or linen; but quite often contributors used the word *linaria* when they were talking about sparto, and vice versa. For these people, *linaria* and *sparto* are polysemantic terms meaning both a plant that produces fabric fibers as well as the woven fabric itself. At present, each seems to be used generically on occasion to mean any bast textile fibers.[19]

Relevant to understanding this system of taxonomy is Brian Morris' study of the way the Chewa of Malwi classify plants (1984). Morris discerned that the Chewa classified plants according to their use; thereby several plants might bear the same folk name. In the same way that the Chewa call various plants "salt" or "poison," so do some Greeks interchange "sparto" and "linaria" to mean a fiber-giving plant.

There are ancient linguistic examples of the interchangeability for "sparto" and "linaria." For instance, Theophrastus (c. 372–287 B.C.) writes of *linosparton* (1.5.2), which a modern translator renders as "Spanish Broom." Modern examples come from statements made by a couple in Krisahori. In 1990, Yorgios (then age seventy-five), showed us a field planted with grapes in which he said he grew sparto until about ten years ago. More likely Yorgios used the term "sparto" generically to mean that he cultivated flax because sparto grows wild in abundance in this area and, in fact, still grows wild along the edge of his field.

Yorgios' wife, Basilike (then age seventy-eight), showed a bedspread that she wove about forty years ago. Basilike's comments added to my understanding of the linen/sparto taxonomy common among rural Greeks: she said sparto fibers were used to make *linaria* to produce the bedspread. This corresponds to another finding of Morris concerning Chewa plant classification wherein the names given to certain plants were the same as the names of their products (1984: 125–7). That is, although Basilike said that she wove with sparto fibers, she called the end-product "*linaria*."[20]

The Chewa and the ancient and modern Greek plant-classifying

systems, and the resulting taxonomies, may be worth considering in translating the Linear B sign *SA*, a sign that has proved troublesome to scholars. Of significance, this particular sign is recorded on the tablets from Pylos (c. 1450 B.C.), a site just adjacent to the geographical boundaries of my own fieldwork, and located in Messinia, a region where wild sparto still grows in abundance.

On the Pylos tablets, the sign for *linon* appears as a heading, under which a place name and personal name are listed followed by the sign *SA* and a number. From the start, *SA* proved a difficult sign to decipher, and in 1973 John Chadwick ambiguously stated:

The attempts that have been made to dissolve the connexion between the ideogram SA and the word re-no=kinon ... have now generally been abandoned. But much doubt still surrounds the meaning of the word linon, since it can refer both to the raw fibers of the flax plant and to the thread and cloth prepared for them ... (Ventris and Chadwick 1973: 468)

SA then was interpreted to mean a weight measurement referring to the flax product (Ibid.: 468–73). Michael Ventris and Chadwick understood that *linon* could relate to the plant as well as to the cloth produced from the plant, but they did not consider the possibility that it might also refer to another plant (sparto) or cloth made from that other plant. All discussion since Ventris and Chadwick has proceeded on the

assumption that *linon* = flax, and that *SA* = weight of flax product (Ventris and Chadwick 1973).[21] Because evidence demonstrates that sparto, as well as linen, were processed into rope and cloth in antiquity, I hypothesize the possibility that "linen" and "sparto" were interchangeable terms in Mycenaean times just as they are now; and that in order to keep sparto products distinct from flax products in the records, the scribes at Pylos inscribed *SA* to mean sparto, not linen. That is, the oldest ancient textual source for sparto may be the Pylos Linear B tablets.

Experts in Linear B coding, however, easily deflect my argument. Cynthia Shelmerdine, for example, explains that in the Linear B syllabary, if a word begins with "s," the "s" is dropped. But in the case of "esparto," the Linear B scribe would have begun the sign with an "e" and not an "s" as in the *SA* sign. I am not arguing, however, that the term "sparto," or even "esparto," was used in Linear B. I am suggesting only that the sign "*SA*" may stand for whatever the Mycenaean term for sparto was, basing my hypothesis on the modern Greek folk taxonomy for identifying the two bast-producing plants—linen and sparto.[22]

Appendix II: Greek Place Names

The modern Greek name *sparto* derives directly from the ancient Greek. In ancient Greek, *sparti* meant rope or cord; *sparton*, rope or cable; *sparton linon*, thread; and, *spartoplokos*, making ropes. This proves the use of the plant's fibers to make rope and other objects. Pliny adopts the Spanish word *esparto*, derived from ancient Greek, when referring to the plant. Pliny had firsthand knowledge of sparto's wide growth and use in Spain, but he furnishes an etymological proof for the ancient Greek use of sparto in rope making and suggests that it was the Greeks who actually taught the Carthaginians its use:

> We may take it on the evidence of the Greek word [meaning rush, rope] that the Greeks used to employ that plant for making ropes; though it is well known that afterwards they used the leaves of palm trees and the inner bark of lime trees. It is extremely probable that the Carthaginians imported the use of esparto grass from Greece. (19.26.9)

Referring to the Italian word "ginestra,"[23] Pliny makes other deductions on the antiquity of the word "sparto" and suggests that Greek native sparto was being used in Homeric times:

> Genista also is used for cords ... I wonder whether this is the plant that Greek writers called sparton because, as I have mentioned, from it the Greeks are wont to make their fishing lines, and whether Homer had it in mind when he said that "the ships' cords (sparto) were loosened" [Iliad 2.135, sparto leluntai]. It is certain that the Spanish or African esparto grass was not yet in use, and though ships were made of sewed seams, yet it was with flax that they were sewed and never with esparto. (24.66.9)

Similar to the antiquity of the word "sparto," the root of the ancient word *linon* for "linen" is retained today as "linaria." The ELPA 1992–3 tourist map book of Greece (in Greek) lists "Linaria" as the name of two villages (1992–3: 232, col. 1). In striking comparison, the ELPA guide lists fifteen villages or towns with "sparto" as the root of the place name (1992–3: 246, col. 3). This suggests that the two plants were associated with, and important to, these places. If so, it also indicates the significance of sparto relative to linen at the time of the naming of the villages and towns.

On the one hand, it might be argued that some villages and towns were named after Sparti, the famous, ancient Greek city-state in Lakonia. On the other hand, it is significant that these other places have names deriving from "sparto," but none replicates the exact name, "sparti." If I am correct in assuming that the fifteen villages and towns received their names from the plant, then one must also ask: what was the importance of this plant to the ancient Spartans?

Tables 1 and 2 list the place names and the provinces in which they are located. The number of place names deriving from "sparto" that are represented in each province is then indicated.

Notes

1. An abbreviated version of this article was published under my former name (Helen Bradley Griebel) in *Textiles in Daily Life* (1992).
2. George Sfikas, however, erroneously makes it a member

Table 1

Place name	Province
Sparto	Attika
Spartera	Kerkouras
Sparti	Lakonia
Spartia	Achaia
Spartia	Kepholonia
Spartia	Lakonia
Spartia	Fthiotida
Spartias	Etolia Akanania
Spartinaika	Korinthios
Sparton	Etolia Akanania
Sparton	Kozani
Spartounta	Hios
Spartohorion	Etolia Akanania
Spartohorion	Leukados
Spatrulas	Kerkuros

Table 2

Province	Number per Province
Stera Ellada (Central Greece and Attika)	5
Ionian Islands	4
Peloponnesos (Achaia, Korinthos, Lakonia)	4
Makedonia (North-central Greece)	1
Nissia Egeou (North-east Agaean Island)	1

of the *Leguminosa*, or Pea, family (1978: 33).

3. Pliny the Elder (first century A.D.) mentions sparto in eight books of his *Natural History*, making his the most extensive coverage of the plant in the ancient records. Pliny went to Spain and names it as the region where the plant grows well: "so far, Gaul is Spain's equal. But it is Spain's deserts that give her the advantage; for here we find esparto grass, selenite and even luxury—in the form of pigments …" (37.203). For the use of esparto in Spain, see Bignia Kuoni (1981).

4. Mary Jaqueline Tyrwhitt writes: "[sparto] has been successfully naturalized on the banks of the [Greek] National Highway, where it looks very handsome when it flowers" (1998: 182).

5. It should be noted that since the 1970s, some form of indoor plumbing has been installed in most rural homes. Streams which formerly were open have been dammed up and rerouted for this purpose, and contributors placed great emphasis on the fact that they no longer have access to running streams in or near their villages in which sparto could be placed to soak.

6. This technique was specifically mentioned by only a few other contributors. On a visit to Kopinaki, her family's village, Greek-American, Amy Kakissis, interviewed her uncle regarding sparto processes. He noted that the dried sparto was boiled before it was soaked for a month in running river water (June 1991). The Peloponnesian Folklore Foundation's exhibition on sparto processing lists the boiling step.

7. Even modern indoor cooking facilities (which few rural Greek kitchens possess) are not equipped to hold a pot large enough to contain the hundreds of stems needed to extract an adequate amount of fiber.

8. In this passage she recounts the beating process as she remembered it from her childhood in the 1950s:

   When the sparto is ready [i.e., after the proper soaking period], the women of the family, the mothers and daughters, beat it. A handful is beaten with the beater (or similar object) in order to peel the stalks … One must be careful not to break the wood of the stalk because afterwards it makes it difficult to separate the fibers. It is very tiring work, we do it from the morning to 8 p.m. and we do it until we finish. Frequently we must go a second day. All the women in the village do this work together, singing a variety of songs recalling the ancient river goddesses, the Nerides, commonly called sea nymphs. A handful is wrung and spread out in the sun to dry. In the evening, the bunches are gathered up and carried on the shoulders homewards, which is a half hour away or thereabouts from the river. (I thank Gigi Cooper and Anthony Aphouras who made the translation from Greek to English.)

9. The Peloponnesian Folklore Museum exhibits a similar tool; the label says it is used to break hemp.

10. While I have no information that sparto fibers were ever used in the Americas, the heckles shown to me by Greek women to comb sparto, flax, and wool are the same as those used in the past in northern Europe and North America to prepare various textile fibers.

11. "Esparto" is the root of the word "espadrille," an inexpensive Spanish shoe made with a cloth top and a rope heel.

12. This contributor is from Velvendo, in the *nomos* Kozani.

13. The loom-woven sparto products I have seen all have

a cotton warp, the spun sparto being used as the weft. The only sparto item listed in the Peloponnesian Folklore Foundation's collection *Catalogue* is a small floor rug with cotton warp and "broom" weft (1981: 61).

14. Thomas Schlereth points out that in less-industrialized societies, individuals are more knowledgeable about who made their work tools than are those in more industrialized societies (1990: 77).

15. See Barbara Kirshenblatt-Gimblett on the retention of material items as objects of memory (1989).

16. Different cultural expectations were observed, however, when Jamie, the visiting American male, joined the women in stripping and cleaning the sparto.

17. Warren Roberts notes that contemporary traditional weavers in Indiana now make their carpets from commercially manufactured rags (1988: 25).

18. For archaeological evidence on the ancient use of flax for textiles, see Helbaek (1959); for woven textiles dating to 8,500 years ago but of as yet unidentified plant fibers, see Helbaek (1963).

19. Tyrwhitt notes, "Flowers tend to be given generic rather than specific names in Greek; all daisy-like ones are *margarita*, all lily-like ones including iris are *krinos*, and the Cruciferae, such as wallflowers and stocks, are all *violtta*" (1998: 140).

20. Just what plant Basilike actually used remains unknown, for the bedspread is softer than other products I have seen woven from sparto, but repeated washing and its age may account for its linen-like texture. It may, however, be woven of flax.

21. E.g., also see Robkin (1979) and Shelmerdine (1981).

22. I thank Professor Shelmerdine, who is unconvinced by my argument, for a valuable conversation on the physical description of *linon* and *SA* as they are found in the Linear B texts.

23. Charles Pickering notes that sparto was "Called in Italy 'ginestra' ... in Greece, 'sparto' ..." (1879: 168).

References

Aristotle. 1936. *Minor Works: Mechanical Problems*. Translated by W.S. Hett. Cambridge, MA: Harvard University Press

Barber, E.J.W. 1991. *Prehistoric Textiles*. Princeton: Princeton University Press.

Clark, M. 1976. "Farming and Foraging in Prehistoric Greece: A Cultural Ecological Perspective." In M. Dimen and E. Friedl (eds.) *Regional Variation in Modern Greece and Cyprus: Toward a Perspective on the Ethnography of Greece* Annals of the New York Academy of Sciences 268, pp. 125–43. New York: The New York Academy of Sciences.

Dioscorides. 1968. *The Greek Herbal* [Illustrated by a Byzantine A.D. 512, Translated by John Goodyear A.D. 1655, Edited and First

Published A.D. 1933] (Facsimile of the 1934 Edition). Edited by R.T. Gunther. London and New York: Hafner.

Dubisch, J. 1986. *Gender and Power in Rural Greece*. Princeton: Princeton University Press.

DuBoulay, J. 1974. *Portrait of a Greek Mountain Village*. Oxford: Oxford University Press.

Dyer, T. 1889. *The Folk-Lore of Plants*. New York: D. Appleton.

ELPA. 1992–3. *Greece: Road and Tourist Maps*. Nineteenth edition. Athens.

Friedl, E. 1962. *Vasilika: A Village in Modern Greece*. New York: Holt, Rinehart and Winston.

Garrad, L.S. 1984. "Some Manx Plant-Lore." In R. Vickery (ed.) *Plant-Lore Studies*, pp. 75–83. London: The Folklore Society.

Gray's Manual of Botany. 1950. Largely written and expanded by M.L. Fernald. New York: American Book Company.

Griebel, H.B. [now, Foster]. 1992. "Sparto: A Greek Textile Plant." In *Textiles in Daily Life: Proceedings of the Third Biennial Symposium of the Textile Society of America*, 179–85.

Helbaek, H. 1959. "Notes on the Evolution and History of Linum." *KUML*: 103–20.

—— 1963. "Textiles from Catal Huyuk." *Archaeology* 16(1): 39–46.

Herodotus. 1957. *The Histories*, Book V. Translated by A.D. Godley. Cambridge, MA: Harvard University Press.

Kirshenblatt-Gimblett, B. 1989. "Objects of Memory: Material Culture as Life Review." In E. Oring (ed.) *Folk Groups and Folklore Genres: A Reader* pp. 329–38. Logan: Utah State University Press.

Koster, J.B. 1976. "From Spindle to Loom: Weaving in the Southern Argolid." *Expedition* 10(1): 29–39.

Kuoni, B. 1981. *Cesteria Tradicional Iberica*, pp. 151–79. Barcelona: Ediciones del Serbal.

Morris, B. 1984. "The Pragmatics of Folk Classifications." In R. Vickery (ed.) *Plant-Lore Studies*, pp. 120–38. London: The Folklore Society.

Morrison, J.S. and J.F. Coates. 1987. *The Athenian Trireme: The History and Reconstruction of an Ancient Greek Warship*. Cambridge: Cambridge University Press.

Museum of Greek Folk Art. n.d. Pamphlet guide. Athens: Ministry of Culture and Sciences.

Pausanias. 1971. *Guide to Greece*, Vol. 2. Translated by Peter Levi. Middlesex: Penguin Books.

Peloponnesian Folklore Foundation. 1981. *Catalogue*. Nafplion, Greece.

Pickering, C. 1879. *History of Plants: Man's Record of His Own Existence Illustrated Through Their Names, Uses, and Companionship*. Boston: Little Brown.

Plato. 1925. *The Statesman*. Translated by H.N. Fowler. London: William Heinemann.

Pliny. 1952. *Natural History*, Vol. IX. Translated by H. Rackham. Cambridge, MA: Harvard University Press.

Roberts, W. 1988. *Viewpoints on Folklife: Looking at the Overlooked*. Ann Arbor, MI: UMI Press.

Robkin, A.L. 1979. "The Agricultural Year, the Commodity *SA* and the Linen Industry of Mycenaean Pylos." *American Journal of Archaeology* 83: 469–74.

Rodd, R. 1892. *The Customs and Lore of Modern Greece*. London: David Stott.

Schlereth, T. 1990. *Cultural History and Material Culture: Everyday Life, Landscapes, Museums*. Ann Arbor, MI: UMI Press.

Sfikas, G. 1978. *Wild Flowers of Greece*. Athens: P. Efstathiadis.

—— 1990. *Trees and Shrubs of Greece*. Athens: Efstathidias Group.

Shelmerdine, C. 1981. "Nichoria in Context: A Major Town in the Pylos Kingdom." *American Journal of Archaeology* 85: 319–25.

Sikeltanos, A. 1988. "The Loom and Greek Popular Culture: Reflections of a Weaver." *Modern Greek Studies Yearbook* 4: 121–30.

Strabo. 1949. *The Geography*. Translated by H.L. Jones. Cambridge, MA: Harvard University Press.

Theophrastus. 1916. *Inquiry Into Plants*. Translated by Sir A. Hort. London: William Heinemann.

Thucydides. 1965. Vol. II. Translated by C.F. Smith. Cambridge, MA: Harvard University Press.

Tyrwhitt, M.J. 1998. *Making a Garden On a Greek Hillside*. Evia, Greece: Denise Harvey.

Ventris, M. and J. Chadwick. 1973. *Documents in Mycenaean Greek*.

Cambridge: Cambridge University Press.

Wace, A. and M. Thompson. 1914. *The Nomads of the Balkans*. London: Methuen.

Widdowson, J.D.A. 1984. "Plants as Elements in Systems of Traditional Verbal Social Control."

In R. Vickery (ed.) *Plant-Lore Studies*, pp. 202–35. London: The Folklore Society.

Xenophon. 1968. Vol. VII: *On Hunting*. Translated by G.W. Bowersock. Cambridge, MA: Harvard University Press.

"Africana" Textiles: Imitation, Adaptation, and Transformation during the Jazz Age

Abstract

Despite centuries of missionary work and trade along the African coasts, not until European colonization at the end of the nineteenth century did African art reach significant levels of visibility in Europe. French interest in Africa gained momentum when Picasso and others witnessed public performances by African-Americans of ragtime music and the cakewalk dance. This exposure led these artists to better appreciate the African sculpture they saw at Parisian flea markets, or in the many world and colonial expositions held after 1900 (Blake 1999). Contact with African music and art then contributed to abstraction in modern art. What began early in the twentieth century was, by the mid-1920s, a full-blown "negrophilia" fueled by jazz music, the Charleston dance, and the Harlem Renaissance (Archer-Straw 2000). Interest in Africa was reflected in the design of everything from furniture, ceramics, and jewelry, to garment styles and textiles (Wood 2003a).

This article examines three ways in which textile artists in Europe and the United States borrowed from African and African-American art sources in order to create "Africana" textiles during the 1920s and 1930s: through imitation, adaptation, and transformation. Imitation occurred when artists borrowed by copying directly from African art. Artists adapted African art patterns to suit their creative and commercial needs, also adapting the energetic sounds of jazz onto textiles perceived to be simultaneously primitive and modern. A third group of artists transformed their source of inspiration, creating images that were the products of Western stereotypes and fantasies long associated with the African landscape, its animals, and its people, rather than images based on African art.

SUSAN HANNEL

Susan Hannel is an Assistant Professor at the University of Rhode Island. She received her Ph.D. from The Ohio State University in the history of clothing and textiles, with supporting emphasis in American history. The research is part of her doctoral dissertation on the influences of both jazz music and African art on textile and fashionable apparel products during the 1920s and 1930s.

Textile, Volume 4, Issue 1, pp. 68–103
Reprints available directly from the Publishers.
Photocopying permitted by licence only.
© 2006 Berg. Printed in the United Kingdom.

"Africana" Textiles: Imitation, Adaptation, and Transformation during the Jazz Age

During the jazz age in Western Europe and the United States, designers in the decorative arts found inspiration among the arts of other cultures, and created new, exotic, and modern products to satisfy the voracious appetites of increasingly sophisticated consumers. Fresh ideas were sought from European folk culture, Egypt, the Middle East, Asia, Native America, Central and South America, but especially Africa. The outcome of these design journeys was a radical shift in the aesthetics of everyday objects, including textiles. African influence made the "primitive" commonplace within Western culture.

African art objects did not reach Europe in numbers significant enough to be influential until the twentieth century. While European trade and missionary work along the coasts of Africa had a long history, widespread European exposure to the African interior did not occur until colonization at the end of the nineteenth century. Thus, European exposure to much of Africa's art occurred only then. As the century turned, African-American musicians and dancers performing in Paris excited interest in Africa. The modern art movement owed much to these influences. Picasso and other artists witnessed public performances by African-Americans of ragtime music and the cakewalk dance in Paris. This exposure made it possible for them to better appreciate the beauty and shape of the African sculpture they saw at Parisian flea markets, or in the many world and colonial expositions held after 1900. Such contact with African music and art eventually contributed to abstraction in modern art (Blake 1999). What began early in the twentieth century was, by the mid-1920s, a full-blown "negrophilia" fueled by jazz music, the Charleston dance, and the Harlem Renaissance (Archer-Straw 2000). This craze for things African, which began during the first part of the 1920s, reached its height with the Colonial Exposition in Paris in 1931.

African themes were particularly adaptable for "Art Moderne" and consequently were re-created in textiles which came to be called "Africana" textiles. Couturiers and artists like Coco Chanel, Elsa Schiaparelli, Madeleine Vionnet, Paul Poiret, and Sonia Delaunay used these textiles for their creations. While ethnic influence on Western textiles in the 1920s is well-established, how influence occurs and why is less well-understood, particularly for Africana textiles. This article focuses on three ways in which artists from the United States and France borrowed African design: through imitation, adaptation, and transformation.

These categories represent three levels of borrowing from African sources. They illustrate the process of design inspiration while simultaneously demonstrating how African influence modified Western textile design. Copies or imitations of African design patterns allowed for rapid responses to this quickly changing visual world. The creators of Africana textiles could swiftly inject modernity into their work by taking design patterns directly from African textiles and sculpture. Adapting rather than copying African art led to textile patterns which retained a visual feeling of primitivism, but also showed the artist's hand and creativity. Adaptation included borrowing geometric shapes associated with African art like triangles, or borrowing rules of visual organization. Adaptation also occurred when the energy of jazz music—music associated with African-Americans and Africans—was reinterpreted for textile surface patterns. The last of the three categories, transformation, is defined here as an alteration in the subject of the patterns chosen for Africana textiles. The subjects were not copied or adapted from patterns found in African art. Instead, the images put onto the textiles were the products of Western stereotypes, myths, and fantasies long associated with the African landscape, its animals, and its people. Because textile artists looked to different sources, the act of transformation occurred in the location of their inspiration. These artists were not copying or adapting African patterns, they were using caricatures for

inspiration and then putting them onto textiles.

Africana textiles became appealing after the First World War when Europeans sought a break with the past by looking to the idea of the primitive as embodied in Rousseau's "Noble Savage," which symbolized a better way to live, one which was simpler and in harmony with nature. At the same time it was believed that art from primitive cultures like those in Africa would replace tired standards of beauty in Western art. The nature of fashion also drove the appeal for Africana textiles. Desires for novelty and change could be satisfied using what were perceived as exotic sources from primitive people and lands. Africana textiles effectively marketed the exotic primitive to fashionable Europeans and Americans. Textile patterns based on African art were highly geometric, with boldly contrasting hues, a style simultaneously labeled "primitive" and "modern." Where the primitive ended and the modern began was unclear. These textile patterns were thought to be appropriate designs for sportswear, a new category of garment also perceived to be the height of modernity. Sportswear included dresses with slim, tubular silhouettes that reiterated the angular patterns found in Africana textiles.

Imitation

To imitate a design requires one to copy it exactly, not varying from the shapes used or the manner in which the shapes are arranged. In addition to being easily and thus quickly rendered, imitation

was part of the urge to re-create and invigorate Western art. In the United States, where there was an ongoing campaign to create a uniquely American style for textiles and apparel based on museum artifacts, African art and textiles became a source of inspiration for American design. As we have seen, African influence was also associated with sportswear, and copies of African textiles were used to market exhibits of African art.

The sudden interest in things African at the start of the 1920s called for quick developments. Textile patterns with designs imitating preexisting African patterns were easier to produce than new patterns, therefore designers were motivated to copy them. The ease of reproduction meant new textiles entered the market more quickly, and speedy textile development allowed for rapid responses to design trends.

Besides being quickly copied in response to changes in artistic trends, African art was also seen as a way of invigorating western art. The *New York Times Magazine* review of the 1923 exhibition Primitive Negro Art stated this was because,

The art of the Congo is little known in this country, and unfavorably known except to a small group of enthusiasts who see in it the source of a new progressive movement in the art of the white man. Their reason for thinking it will be progressive is, to speak quite seriously, their knowledge of the limitations of the negro [sic] mind, of the fact that the negro [sic] mind beyond a

Figure 1
Congo Cloth, from Crawford (1923b).
Courtesy of Brooklyn Museum of Art,
Culin Archival Collection.

SCHIFFLI EMBROIDERIES INSPIRED BY PRIMITIVE NEGRO MOTIFS

Series of Patterns in Congo Cloth Representing Modern Adaptations of Designs From
Sleeping Mats Used in the Huts of African Negroes. (See text on opposite page.)
Designed and Manufactured by Blanck & Co., Inc.

*certain point rejects instruction,
is inaccessible to scholarship,
remains primitive, and therefore
keeps basic ideas which are not
frittered away by the invasion
of supplementary, superficial,
extraneous ideas. (1923: 12)*

Primitive Negro Art was one of
the first exhibits displaying African
objects as art in the United States.
The exhibit was devoted to artifacts
from the Bushong in what was
then the Belgian Congo, now the
Democratic Republic of the Congo.
The Brooklyn Museum's curator of
ethnology, Stewart Culin, marketed
the exhibition in a manner unique
for the time, commissioning
artists to create designs based on
the Bushong artifacts. Dress and
upholstery textiles were among the
blankets, pillows, garments, hats,
wooden carvings, and dolls that

resulted from their efforts. 'Congo Cloth' (Figure 1) was a cambric textile with embroidered designs copied from patterns found in the raffia sleeping and burial mats by artists of the Bushong. Congo Cloth was formed into hats and sewn into dresses labeled "Sports Attire," created by designers at Bonwit Teller and sold there, as well as at the Brooklyn Museum (Figure 2).

The Bonwit Teller window display blurred the boundaries between the authenticity of museum artifacts and the commercial world. The uniqueness of the African textiles was maintained yet modernized for use in sports dresses. Here, African authenticity was linked to the originality of the resulting products. Culin praised the Fifth Avenue display of the dresses. "The window is unique in the world and worth going far to see. No museum can touch it" (pers. corr.). The display of dresses was new, one-of-a-kind, and consequently authentically "modern." Thus, authentic African designs were the source for authentic, unique, and modern garment designs.

While the creation of Congo Cloth was primarily a way of marketing an exhibition of African art and thus linking African art to the consumer habits of the American public, it was also a late entry in the race to develop an American design style. The movement to create uniquely American designs began when the First World War threatened to cut off French sources of inspiration. American textile and clothing manufacturers sought to create an American style based primarily on designs from Peruvian and Native American artifacts found in American museums, but also on designs from African artifacts. Morris De Camp Crawford, design editor for the apparel trade paper, *Women's Wear*, and an honorary research assistant in textiles for the American Museum of Natural History, became one of the leaders of this American style movement.

During the First World War Crawford was approached by the editor of *Women's Wear*, W. Fairchild, to consider the problem of America's dependence on French design. Along with other industry leaders like Albert Blum, treasurer of the United Piece Dye Works and a partner in a Lyonaise dye house, Crawford and Fairchild explored the possibility of textile artists and clothing designers using museum collections in the United States as inspiration

Figure 2
Congo Cloth used for dresses sold by Bonwit Teller. "Cotton Frocks Shown by Bonwit Teller & Co. Related in Design to African Art." *Women's Wear*, 20(8) (April 14, 1923).

for their creations rather than copying French examples. The curators of the museums in New York City and Brooklyn were enthusiastic supporters and made their collections accessible to the artists. Crawford then launched a forceful media campaign focused primarily on the industry via articles and advice in *Women's Wear*, but also aimed at the general public through books, popular magazines, and newspapers like *House Beautiful* and the *New York Tribune. Women's Wear* also sponsored textile design competitions.

In 1919 Crawford was particularly enthusiastic about a cretonne fabric of cotton and jute printed with a design by Martha Ryther based on, but not a copy of, the embroidered pocket of a 'Congo burnous' (Crawford 1919: 42). At that time Crawford was not a fan of textile patterns that imitated the arts of other cultures, believing that, "Often the best designs, both from the artistic and the commercial standpoint are the ones in which the museum influence is rather of inspiration than of emulation" (Ibid.: 16). Crawford thought it important that the source of inspiration for the textile was obscure. Unfortunately, the uniqueness of the Ryther design led to poor sales. He thought the problem was the lack of familiarity with the style, and surmised that it would sell if it were offered directly to the public: "I believe the first victory for modern ornament must be won over professional inertia to novelty, not over public taste" (Ibid.: 42). From Crawford's point of view, the American public was more

accepting of new designs than was the textile manufacturing industry.

By 1923 Crawford seemed to have either altered his opinion about contemporary copies of museum artifacts, or was determined to promote the exhibition, Primitive Negro Art. In praising the origins of Congo Cloth, Crawford argued that "It is an ingenious source of inspiration, and the designs and colorings may also be termed ingenious for they are an exact duplication in appearance if not in materials" (1923b). He supported the copies created by American artists because they were ingenious. By using the word "ingenious," Crawford is alluding to "American ingenuity," a phrase often linked with the acumen of American business.

There was some ambivalence about using African sources for American textile design. Crawford preferred the primitive art of the New World due to its richness and boldness of design, and because he believed it was not connected to European textile traditions and contemporary developments. At this time Europe was more interested in African ethnographic arts and the exotics of the East (Wood 2003a, b). Crawford avoided promoting European trends (Whitley 1994).

Crawford's ambivalence was evident in the paucity of his praise for African-inspired creations compared to his praise for art from other cultures. In a 1916 article for *Women's Wear* (December 11), Crawford included a simple line drawing of a raffia mat in "black and dull yellow" from the "Bakuba" in the Congo, one of the earliest examples of African textiles suggested as inspiration for modern sportswear fabrics. While in the accompanying article Crawford suggested that, "This design and many others of the same series have remarkable qualities for sports fabrics," and it "is good beyond all praise," never far from this praise was Crawford's underlying discomfort with its origins. He made a point of noting that the pattern may have come from "Arabian" basketry. When he admitted that "it is rather doubtful that such a fact could be proved," it becomes clear that he was trying to give the work legitimacy as all things Arabian and Oriental were more acceptable, despite the disputable facts. The pattern on the raffia mat does not seem to have stood on its own merit. Crawford concluded with resoundingly ambivalent praise: "in spite of its origin and the crudity of the civilization from which it comes, it would have done Bakst great credit had he produced it" (Ibid.).

Crawford's commentary for *Women's Wear* about the 1923 exhibit of African art at the Brooklyn Museum made his preference clear despite the compliments to the art: "The African material, while not so highly developed nor so intricate as the arts of Asia or southern Europe, still has much in its vigorous simplicity and spirited drawing to attract the designer of these times" (1923a: 31). He stated that the arts of the native people from the Belgian Congo show "more than a suggestion of Egyptian Modeling and Design in Human and Animal Figures" (Ibid.), and Bushong thrones specifically

"are almost certain proof of contact with a superior race, perhaps Egyptian" (1923: 28). Crawford was again trying to legitimize the origins of the Congo textiles by linking them to Egypt. He did give the work credit for having "a high artistic sense" and "outclassing" the art of Polynesia compared to all of the other "exotic arts" (1923a: 31).

This ambivalence toward African artifacts had its origins in mainstream racism. One would have had difficulty marketing to White America a product which was inspired by Africa, a culture whose descendants living in America were often viewed as ignorant, unintelligent, and incapable of art. The shift in attitudes came later in the 1920s when the French craze for jazz music, an African-American art form the French simultaneously linked with African sculpture, gave it cultural legitimacy (Blake: 1999).

Eight years after the Brooklyn Museum's exhibit of African art, the American textile manufacturing firm, Mallinson and Co. Inc., produced a series of printed silks with "Barbaric Themes" inspired by the Exposition Coloniale held that year in Paris (Figure 3). The 1931 Exposition Coloniale Internationale was the most famous and internationally influential of the many colonial expositions after 1906. Held between May and November in the Bois de Vincennes outside Paris, the Exposition Coloniale's mission was to educate the French people about their colonies and create support for colonization. While the Exposition's mission to create support for colonization has since been considered unsuccessful by

colonial scholars, over 33 million people saw the exhibits displayed there. One can surmise that these large attendance numbers would lead to some influence on the decorative arts, including textile design.

The North African displays at the Exposition Coloniale were quite familiar to the French, who had seen similar displays at the many previous expositions due to the French colonial presence in Algeria since the 1830s. Less familiar were the displays by West Indian and Central African nations, colonies which had only been acquired since the First World War. These displays had more exotic appeal because of their novelty and perceived relationship to the African descendants playing American jazz in Parisian nightclubs. Fashionable Parisians and the international social set wanted to "go native" because it was the "in thing" to do (Chandler 1990: 93–4). The Exposition inspired the Comte and Comtesse Étienne de Beaumont to give a costume ball called the "Fête Coloniale," where the couturier, Chanel, came "as a nigger sailor boy" and "Madame Eloui Bey, surrounded by a contingent of young men dressed like members of the Foreign Legion, danced in the fantastic and gaudy costume of a woman in an African boîte frequented by lonely légionnaires" (*Vogue* October 15, 1931: 102).

While the goal to create support for colonialism was unrealized, the 1931 Exposition Coloniale Internationale did reinforce the tendency toward exoticism and Orientalism already present in fashion. The page of print designs

Figure 3
Textile patterns by Mallison and
Co. inspired by the 1931 Exposition
Coloniale in Paris (American Silk
Journal 1931: 40). From top, left
to right: Temple of Angkor, Togo,
Madagar, Marrakech, Timbuktu, New
Caledonia, and Ubanghi.

BARBARIC THEMES IN NEW SEASON SILKS

for the Mallinson silks is an example of the kind of exoticism that existed in the decorative arts in Europe and North America at the time of the exposition. All seven textile print designs by Mallinson were copies of textiles, or interpretations of the art from the indigenous cultures in the French colonies (*American Silk Journal*, November 1931: 40). "The Temple of Angkor" (Cambodia) and "New Caledonia" (in the Southwest Pacific) are the only two prints based on textiles from cultures outside of Africa. There are two North African prints, "Marrakech" (Morroco), and "Madagar," from Madagascar, the name of a large island off Africa's southeast coast with strong East Asian cultural influence. Three prints were copied from sub-Saharan African textiles. "Togo" was "a primitive design symbolic of Togoland, a French colony in West Africa." "Timbuktu," named for a city in the West African country of Mali, was "an impressionistic design of this African colony as depicted at the Paris Exposition." "Ubanghi," one of the major tributaries in the Congo, was "a design of pure African origin" (Ibid.).

"Barbaric" was used to indicate the range of cultures like those encompassed by the Mallinson silks and was one of many words that communicated the "exotic." American fashion magazines called any non-western form of adornment "barbaric." The Kabyle women, Berbers from Morroco, wore "barbaric jewelry of silver and coral or red beeswax" (Stewart 1924: 134). At a wedding in Biskra, Algeria, there was "a great deal of barbaric ornaments in gold and silver" (Sheridan 1935: 82, 84).

Exoticism and the spectrum of cultural borrowing were also illustrated when African triangular shapes were incorporated into textile patterns. Triangles in high contrast colors like black and white were appealing because they conveyed modernity through a specific type of exoticism called primitivism. The current art historical definition of primitivism describes it as a modern, predominantly Western phenomenon. Primitivism in art occurs when artists interested in tribal art and culture express that interest in their ideas and artwork (Rubin 1984). Art historians have considered primitive art only since the Second World War. The word was first used in an art-historical way during the nineteenth century to illustrate the influence on painting and sculpture by artists known as primitives, mostly Flemish and Italian painters from the fourteenth and fifteenth centuries, including Romanesque and Byzantine painters but

also generally any non-Western artist. During this period in the nineteenth century the term did not include any reference to African or Oceanic art (Rubin 1984: 2). It was later defined in an American dictionary as "a belief in the superiority of primitive life" and a desire to return to the land, both ideas connected to Rousseau's image of the Noble Savage. The art-historical definition at that time was "the adherence to or reaction to that which is primitive" (*Webster*, 1934 as quoted in Rubin 1984: 2).

Artists at the end of the nineteenth century, who felt stifled by the salon art of the day, used words like "primitive" and "savage" in an admiring way to describe non-Western art which ranged from that of Egypt, the Aztecs, Japan, Persia, India, Java, Cambodia, to Peru. At the beginning of the 1920s, the use of the word "primitivism" in fashion magazines adhered to older art-historical definitions. Thus, in 1923 primitive influence in fashionable textiles included Romanian embroidery in black and white (*Harper's Bazar*, April 1923a: 63).

African and Oceanic arts were not categorized as primitive until the early twentieth century, when artists like Picasso, Matisse, Derain, and Vlaminck began to see the art in curiosity shops and flea markets, and gave it a more modernist interpretation (Rubin 1984). The Parisians used the terms "art nègre" and "primitive art" synonymously to mean both the arts of Africa and Oceania. During the 1920s primitive art came to mean only the tribal art of Africa and Oceania and no longer

included Japanese, Egyptian, Persian, Cambodian, and other non-Western arts. By the 1930s that meaning had been solidified. A 1931 textile print designed by a university student was based on animal forms and geometric figures used by "primitive man" in Africa and Hawaii (Oceania) (Rhodes 1930b: 70). The common link between the earlier, broader definitions of primitivism in textile design, and later more narrowly defined examples was the graphic, geometric nature of the designs, qualities that were also described as "modern" because hard edges and geometric shapes reflected the appearance of modern machinery and buildings.

The appeal of using basic geometric shapes from African sources is made evident in a 1924 coat designed and modeled by Sonia Delaunay with patterned bands of highly contrasting dark and light "Africanized angles" around the neck, opening, hem, and sleeves (Damase 1991: 143). Triangular shapes were among those seen in the Bushong culture. Buckberrough (1995: 51–5) interpreted the Africanizing elements of Delaunay's work as one part of the avant-garde design aesthetic which sought to change life for the bourgeoisie: "Delaunay's aesthetic urged reconsideration of one's place in the world—in sympathy with cultural migrations, collisions, mergers, reformulations—and recognized a progressive bourgeois right to support, through aesthetic presence, the world's dynamic state of change" (Ibid.: 55). Delaunay's abstracted and primitivistic patterns were

Figure 4
Dress with textile pattern influenced
by Nyoro pattern. Drawing based on
photo by P. Géniaux. Photo archives,
UFAC- Louvre, Paris, France.

meant to reflect the increased freedom or "wildness" and "savagery" of the modern women, two words and ideas that, like "barbaric," signified the exotic. Delaunay's designs also reflected the movement and speed of the modern world.

The simultaneous reference to the hard-edged modern world and vibrant African designs is shown in a pattern of long, narrow triangles arranged horizontally in a dress fabric worn by the French woman in Figure 4. The design in the fabric clearly and convincingly imitates the patterns in Figure 5 found on a pot stand from the Nyoro culture in Uganda. The sharp edges and high contrast between black and white make the textile vibrate with visual energy. The textile pattern's edges and sense of movement in Figure 4 also contribute to the masculinity of the tubular dress silhouette. Masculinity in women's fashions was attributed by Poiret to the American influence in France so prevalent in the second half of the 1920s (1927: 32–3), and considered one aspect of the modern female savage. Therefore the choice of a "savage" African pattern would be appropriate.

The Nyoro-copied print design also mimics the striped patterns found in zebra fur. The black and white striped fur of the African zebra was very much associated with the "Africana Craze" (Hannel 2002). Zebra skins, and textile prints based on the fur pattern, became popular for clothing and interiors, emerging in the 1920s as one of the most cogent symbols of exotic modernity (Woods 2003a). Zebra was used for a "barbaric-looking collar" in a 1922 evening wrap, which also included monkey trim, the entire wrap creating "a most exotic effect" (*Harper's Bazar*, October 1922: 46–7). The French couturiers Talbot, Lelong, and Molyneux all decorated their homes with zebra skins (*Harper's Bazar*, February 26, 1926: 54, August 1928: 64–5; *Vogue*, January 15, 1931: 66–7).

Chanel was one of many Parisian couturiers and artists who utilized African shapes and patterns, particularly triangular shapes, in textiles. Chanel chose jersey fabric with triangular

Figure 5
Pattern on pot stand from the Nyoro
culture, Uganda (from Williams 1971:
61).

shapes from African sources for a coat dress in her spring 1930 line (Figure 6). The textile was "known as the most costly fabric in the collection" (de Meyer 1930: 124). The black triangular shapes were copied from Kuba textiles found in South Central Democratic Republic of the Congo and maintain the feeling of the original textile (Figure 7). As early as 1916 Crawford was suggesting African patterns as appropriate for sportswear and that "'Bakuba' might easily become a descriptive trademark for sports fabrics" (1916). He again linked African textiles to sportswear in 1923 with the promotion of "Congo Cloth" as an appropriate fabric for "sports apparel for the modern woman" (1923b).

The couturier Paul Poiret also incorporated textile patterns of African-inspired triangles. In 1922 he designed an evening coat with a surface pattern of extremely long, pointed triangles similar to the long triangular shapes painted on bark cloth from the Baganda of Uganda in East Africa (Poiret Archives, UFAC-Louvre; Coquet 1998: pl. 124). A 1928 Vionnet dress had a pattern of applied beads in irregular shapes of triangles, rhomboids, and rectangles, similar to the patterns found in batik raffia women's cloth from the Ivory Coast (*Harper's Bazar*, November 1928: 102; Coquet 1998: pl. 31).

Adaptation

Creating direct copies of African art could be especially frustrating for artists who sought to be original, therefore many artists chose to adapt African designs rather than copy them. In order to suit the geometric style of Art Moderne, these adaptations drew on the same triangular forms and geometric motifs for inspiration as did textile

Figure 6
Textile inspired by Kuba culture, Democratic Republic of the Congo, 1930. Dress by Chanel (Baron de Meyer 1930: 610).

Figure 7
Textile from Kuba culture, Democratic Republic of the Congo, with pile and embroidery in raffia. Courtesy of The Rhode Island School of Design Museum.

patterns that were copies of African designs. Adaptation also included borrowing rules of visual organization from African cultures, as well as translating African musical influences like jazz into two dimensions. Much of the influence of African art and textiles developed into a general feeling of primitivism in Western textile design.

Adapting instead of copying African textile and art patterns served many purposes. Altering sources of inspiration was part of the creative process. For the textile designer, to adapt a pattern from an African source was to make it their own and create something unique. People working in the apparel trade got ideas for African-inspired print design in many places. In the United States *Women's Wear* featured a full-page illustration of African textiles and themes to accompany the opening of the 1923 Brooklyn Museum exhibit, Primitive Negro Art (Crawford 2003a: 31). It is logical to assume this large illustration would have had some influence on textile designers.

The years 1925 to 1931 saw the most significant numbers of African-influenced textiles. "Smart women in Paris" were wearing sportswear in fabrics printed, appliquéd, and painted with geometric patterns based on raffia appliquéd dancing skirts for Kuba/Ngongo women in the Congo (Figures 8 and 9), the linear motifs from Bunnu Yoruba (Nigeria) funeral cloth (*Harper's Bazar*, September 1923: 66; Idiens and Ponting 1980. 86), and resist-dyed raffia, also from the Kuba people (Fashion photo archive,

UFAC-Louvre; Picton and Mack 1989: 149).

Like Delaunay, Chanel, Poiret, and Vionnet, the couturier Elsa Schiaparelli used textiles with patterns copied directly from African art, as well as interpreting or abstracting those influences. Schiaparelli adopted the "savage colours and forms" of the African sculpture seen at the 1922 French Colonial Art Exhibition in her hand-knitted sweaters as well as "masks and idols from various countries in French Equatorial Africa, and magical symbols from the French Congo" (Herald 1991: 41; White 1986: 62, 146). In 1928 Schiaparelli again created hand-knitted sweaters with patterns inspired by African Negro art (Figure 10). *Harper's Bazar* described them thus:

Barbaric designs showing the direct influence of their African Negro origin have been cleverly employed by Schiaparelli in a new line of sports sweaters. The effect of these sweaters is unusual and exciting. This one is in handknitted wool, rather heavy in quality. It is black and white, with its elaborate negro art design standing out boldly against the black foundation. (December 1928: 81)

In her biography Schiaparelli says about the sweaters that "she added Negro-like designs of her own, and strange scrawls from the Congo" (1954: 64). The linear designs on the sweaters bear some resemblance to Kuba men's dancing skirts (Figure 11). The sweater is interesting for its adoption of African themes, but more significant is its placement

Figure 8
Brown tweed textile appliquéd with pattern similar to appliquéd raffia dancing skirts worn by Kuba woman, Democratic Republic of the Congo (*Harper's Bazar* 1927: 126).

in Figure 10 beside sweaters with geometric patterns labeled "modern." The "modern" and the "barbaric" were placed side by side, thus reinforcing the place African art had in the design of modern textile patterns.

Schiaparelli's interest in Africa was perhaps sparked when she was quite young. In her autobiography she spins a tale about a frightening "Zulu" nurse hired to take care of her as a small child: "She was a terrifying person—very black, bony, tall, with a mop of short white hair, a foretaste of the 1920 craze for bobbed hair. Holding a flickering candle, she would come noiselessly into my dark bedroom to say good night. She would sit at the foot of my bed and whisper: 'I love you so much. I have buried all the people I have loved. I want to bury you too'" (Schiaparelli 1954: 15). The story is quite fanciful while conveying stereotypes of

Figure 9
Raffia appliquéd textile, Kuba/Ngongo or Maluk culture, Democratic Republic
of the Congo. Courtesy of The Rhode Island School of Design Museum.

SCHIAPARELLI   JANE REGNY

Figure 10
Center: sweater by Schiaparelli inspired by "African Negro art" (*Harper's Bazar* 1928 c: 81).

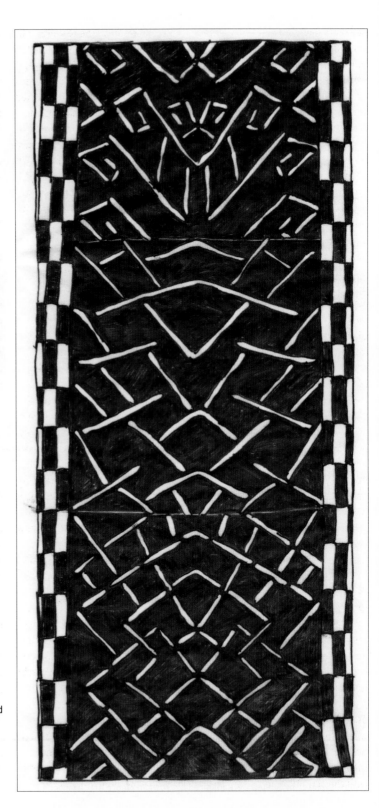

Figure 11
Kuba men's dancing skirt in raffia
from the Kasai region, Democratic
Republic of the Congo. Drawing based
on photograph in Clark (1998: 57).

savagery and violence associated with Africans. Yet, it is also meant to illustrate Schiaparelli's unique experiences, including early encounters with "real" Africans leading her eventually to adopt African motifs in the fabrics for her apparel. The tale is also about her fearlessness in frightening situations and her fearless creativity.

Africa clearly was a source of inspiration which Schiaparelli came back to from time to time, particularly for her "barbaric" and "ferocious" jewelry in 1932 and in 1935 (Vogue, December 1, 1932: 51; Harper's Bazaar, May 1935: 94–5). By 1938 she was displaying her non-African-derived jewelry on an African reliquary sculpture (Vogue, October 15, 1938: 23). The sculpture was from the Pahouin people in Northern Gabon and had been exhibited at the African Negro Art exhibit at the Museum of Modern Art in New York in 1935.[2] The eye-catching advertisement had no caption other than "Schiaparelli Jewelry" but says much about the popularity of African art, and by association provides insight into the emergence of Africana textiles.

The advertisement illustrates the elevated popularity and chicness of African art by 1938. To be primitive was to be fashionable and modern. Such an advertisement had the capacity to make non-African-inspired jewelry fashionable. It also rendered primitive that which was not primitive. Or perhaps the primitive was to be made modern with Schiaparelli jewelry. The viewer of the advertisement would identify with the sculpture because she too would be wearing the jewelry. If the sculpture represented what was then perceived as a wild savage, and the wild savage could be made fashionable with this jewelry, then so could the viewer. That such an association could be drawn on to sell jewelry says much about both the popularity of African art and the power of a couturier to "sell" the primitive image as a fashionable identity for women in the West by the end of the 1930s.

However, in 1925 the use of primitive African sources for artistic inspiration was just beginning to gain momentum. In that year basic geometric shapes taken from Congolese textile patterns were being used in freshman design classes at the University of Washington in Seattle. Disturbed by the plethora of "holly, peacocks and butterflies" that design students were using to create interpretive motifs, their instructor, Helen Rhodes, turned to textile patterns from the Congo (1925: 1–4). She gave the students basic shapes taken from African patterns (Figure 12), and asked them to create a repetitive pattern. One of the resulting designs is seen in Figure 13. Rhodes found the results strong and individual, not the "ready-made formula[s]" she disparaged: "The basic aim, therefore, of our teaching in Design [sic] today must be the arousing of interest in individual and original self-expression, making the sterile reproduction of pretty motifs or repeats as distasteful to the student as it is to most teachers" (Ibid.: 1). In particular, she thought the students developed a finer sense of light and dark in pattern.

While the University of Washington student designs were not intended for the textile market, Rhodes felt textile manufacturers would find the work acceptable. She again promoted the use of the geometric shapes and animal figures from primitive African cultures in 1930 for the decorative arts journal, Design, when the entire May issue was devoted to African art (Design 1930: 18–19). The issue included several photos of African textiles, as well as recycled images of the student work from Rhodes' 1925 article promoting the use of African motifs to teach design. Rhodes took a different tack in 1930, explaining why she felt employing primitive art should be used both to learn design analysis and as a source of inspiration for design students. Because, in her opinion only the best of it had been preserved, African art was helpful for studying the basic design laws of rhythm, variety, subordination, opposition, and unity. All the laws were present in African art and therefore more easily visible when compared to some forms of Western art. Rhodes also believed that "the impulse of joy and play and spontaneity is close to the aesthetic impulse of the primitive" (1930a: 18). She felt working with African motifs encouraged students to have the same approach to their creative process. Arguing the benefits of the simplicity of African art, as well as its childlike qualities, while presumably a positive influence on design students, also tapped into common negative racial stereotypes associated with African art and artists. Finally, Rhodes was quite disdainful of "the merely pretty or superficial," arguing that:

Figure 12
Shapes taken from African textiles to
be used by beginning design students.
From Rhodes (1925: 1–4).

Figure 12
Shapes taken from African textiles to
be used by beginning design students.
From Rhodes (1925: 1–4).

*The design of the primitive
artist was* strong, virile, *rarely
weak or decadent. Useless
lines and a superficial quality
are never found in it. Many
primitive textile designs are
founded on simple geometric
forms in original and strong
combinations. It is this feeling
for* strength, simplification *and*
abstraction *or* generalization,
*with a desire for originality and
self-expression, which the art
teacher knows will obliterate the
false ideals of beauty which
the students have acquired.*
(Ibid.: 19)

Rhodes' comments reflect the
changing attitudes toward what
constituted good art, good design,
and perceptions of beauty. Using
African art to illustrate and create
this emerging visual world was
part of the break with the past
begun by the tragedy of the First

World War. The aftermath of the
war led to a critique of Western
civilization at the center of which
stood Africa: "the dreadful,
mechanical slaughter of the war
sharply increased this fascination,
for African culture seemed to
embody the lush, naïve sensuality
and spirituality that cold, rational
Europeans had lost" (Stovall 1996:
31). Europe embraced the myth of
Rousseau's "noble savage," seeing
African people as not equal, but
rather as innocent and uncorrupted
with a proximity to nature that
rendered them superior to white
Europeans.

The adaptation of African art
was not limited to the manipulation
of shapes and lines. The aesthetic
rules governing all-over patterns
were also manipulated. The
adaptation of the rules governing
Ghanaian Kente/Asante cloth
provides a valuable example. Kente
cloth has narrow strips of fabric

Figure 13
Design created by University of
Washington art student, Mary
McEacheran, based on African shapes
in Figure 12. From Rhodes (1925:
1–4).

sewn together in such a way that identical shapes in the woven pattern do not always appear to line up across the finished fabric. Sonia Delaunay created a design for a textile which clearly borrowed the strip-like structure of Kente cloth (Damase 1991: 135). However, Delaunay did make changes. Instead of shifting the placement of identical patterns, as was done in Ghanaian textiles to create visual energy and a sense of being off-balance, she used identical diamond shapes situated next to one another from strip to strip. To create visual energy Delaunay utilized color shifts within the diamonds from strip to strip. She chose colors—browns, bronze, beige, and black—associated with primitive materials. The use of natural materials like wooden beads to embellish garments and the use of hues found in natural materials were trends associated with the interest in primitive cultures. For instance, the range of textile colors for Madame Agnès' 1926 hats inspired by Mangbetu hair and head shapes were described as "couleurs nègres," rust, brown, beige, and "high yellow" (*Harper's Bazar*, July 1926: 80).

Patterns for striped and plaid woolens also appear to have borrowed from the rules applied to Asante textiles. A 1931 suit by Premet was sewn in a wool plaid where panels of varying widths contained narrow stripes. From panel to panel the stripes within the panels shifted direction from vertical to horizontal. The result was a highly graphic, visually rhythmic textile that adapted the strip-like structure of Kente cloth and the idea of pattern shifts, if not the exact manner in which patterns are shifted. The effects were increased graphic quality, as well as visual energy and movement.

The graphic quality of drawnwork from Buguma, Nigeria (Figure 14), appears to have been the inspiration for the wool fabric in Figure 15. A fabric with a similar pattern was illustrated in 1926 for a coat and dress ensemble (*Vogue*, March 1, 1926: 104). Again, the result of the pattern is highly geometric and graphic, and thus would have been perceived as extremely modern. The pattern in the wool also encompasses the fashion for black and white stripes like those seen in the fur of the African zebra, previously illustrated in the dress with the Nyoro pattern (Figure 4).

The process of adaptation in Africana textiles included translating the energetic qualities of the popular jazz dances of the era like the Charleston into textile patterns. The connection between Africa and the Charleston was formed by the African-American performers who created the music and initiated the dance. As with the earlier cakewalk and its influence on French artists' appreciation of African sculpture, African-Americans playing jazz or performing the Charleston during the 1920s in New York City's Harlem, and Montmartre in Paris, continued to excite as well as fuel general interest in primitivism and African art.

Poiret felt that the American influence in France was very strong in 1927 and, "Even more American [than the interest in wealth and money, cigarettes, and masculine silhouettes for women like those found in pajama pants] are the implacable and hypertrophic rhythms of the new dances, the blues and the Charlestons, the din of unearthly instruments, and the musical idioms of exotic lands" (Poiret 1927: 32). Woods affirms that "jazz came to simultaneously symbolize the exotic and modern urban living. The parallels between the complex patterns of jazz and the energetic geometric forms of Art Deco were clear, and as a result the style was often known as 'Jazz Moderne'" (Wood 2003b: 135).

Many textiles were printed with dancing figures and given the name "Charleston." Some textiles labeled "Charleston" utilized triangles and other geometric shapes associated with African art. Delaunay's 1925 sketch of her "Charleston" garment illustrates this point well because the garment had an hourglass shape created by joining the points of two triangles at the waist. The textile design for the dress contained rows of black and white triangles (Damase 1991: 105). One could argue that the severe, jumpy triangles in the textile for the French dress in Figure 4 illustrate not just the influence of Nyoro pottery and zebra stripes, but also the strong rhythmic feeling of syncopated jazz music.

Transformation

The adaptation of African art patterns and jazz music's energy and rhythms into Africana textiles are approaches to the process of borrowing artistic influences.

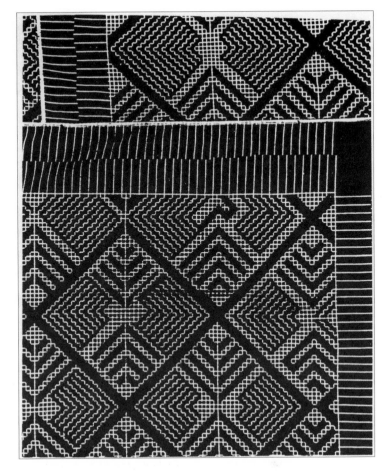

Figure 14
Drawnwork from Buguma, Nigeria.
From Eicher (1976: 92).

Transformation is the last type of borrowing considered in this article. Transformation, defined as changing the character or condition of a motif or pattern, is the ultimate goal of the creative process. However, here prints in Africana textiles transformed African themes rather than African motifs. While these Africana textiles reflected primitivism and exoticism like those that copied or adapted motifs, they appealed to people who experienced specific exotic dreams or fantasies about primitive African people, wild African animals, and tropical landscapes. Many of these textiles were appealing because they relied on pictorial representations rather than abstracted forms, satisfying the need for exotic themes without appearing overly geometric and modern.

Two series of Africana textiles, the "Zanbaraza" line by C.K. Eagle Co. and the "Safari Silks" line by Belding-Heminway, demonstrate which exotic subjects were thought to be marketable in the United States. The *American Silk Journal* promoted the use of African artifacts in 1929 and 1930, a continuation of earlier attempts to develop an American design style, by reporting on the cooperation between textile firms and the design students at Ethel Traphagen's School of Fashion. The students' designs were inspired by the artifacts Traphagen collected on a trip to Africa in 1928. Traphagen's husband, William R. Leigh, was an artist commissioned by the American Museum of Natural History to accompany Carl Akeley's last African expedition in 1926 (Barton 1929: 48–9). Traphagen, upon seeing the artifacts her husband had collected, was "at once fired with

Figure 15
Black and white wool plaid. University of Rhode Island Historic Textiles and Costume Collection, Tirocchi Collection
(90.10.301).

the wealth of artistic inspiration," which led her to join him for a second expedition where "she was determined to bring back the most comprehensive collection of art Africana in America" (*American Silk Journal*, 1930: 39–40). The design students then used this collection, which included native African dress, to create about 300 African designs. After a two-month exhibition, a prize was awarded for the best design, and some of the student designs were chosen for the line of prints called "Zanbaraza," produced by the C.K. Eagle Co. The name of the textile line, Zanbaraza, like the

textiles it represented, was a transformation of the word, Zanzibari, an adjective describing anything from the island of Zanzibar, off the east coast of Africa (Ibid.).

Traphagen was applauded for her tutelage of her design students, as well as her desire to create a truly American style. She was:

forever doing notable things to gain for the textile and other industries of her own country, independence in the art of fashioning women's wear and other articles of domestic

*use, had more in mind than
merely creating the African
silk motif, which has recently
taken such a substantial hold
upon our people. She saw in
this major fashion movement
the beginning of the end in our
habitual search for adequate
dress design abroad. To
Miss Traphagen, a slavish
dependence upon Europe
for dress and other design
was the most senseless and
intolerable condition in current
American art. To her it seemed
to be as unnecessary as it was
undesirable. She believed that
so long as we depended upon
Europe for our art designs, art
objects and the pictorial, plastic
and manual arts, the great body
of American artists would never
attain the position in the world
to which its impressive talents
entitle it—have long ago entitled
it. (Ibid.: 40)*

She was also erroneously
credited with being the first
person to bring African design
to American fashion:

*Until then not a word had been
publicly uttered, nor a single
African design displayed in
what promises to be a new era
in American fashions. It was
Ethel Traphagen alone and the
several hundred pupils inspired
by her teaching, her precept
and example, who founded the
African motif which is imparting
such color and vivacity to
women's wear in the new year.
(Ibid.)*

Obviously the above
paragraph is marketing spin.

At least two examples pre-date
Traphagen's work. The silhouette
and embroidery of a Hausa
garment from Nigeria inspired a
1917 negligee by Jessie Franklin
Turner (Crawford 1917: 5). The
aforementioned "Congo Cloth"
textiles produced for the Primitive
Negro Art exhibit at the Brooklyn
Museum in 1923 (Figure 1) also pre-
date Traphagen's efforts.

The textile designs created
by Traphagen students appeared
in the *American Silk Journal*
(1930a: 49). All the prints
were interpretations of the
African landscape rather than
interpretations of African art. The
work showed much interest in
palm trees, elephants, monkeys,
and giraffes. There were warriors
brandishing spears, mothers with
their children, and grass huts that
framed black figures, and a map of
Africa.

Dresses designed by former
Traphagen student, George Knox, a
well-known designer by 1930, were
also shown because the print of
one dress replicated the pattern in
an African basket. These designs
were seen as "really American,"
presumably because they were
created by an American (Barton
1929: 48). The contradiction of
using African themes to create
"American" textile patterns seems
lost on the author.

At the same time as the C.K.
Eagle Co. was promoting its
"Zanbaraza" prints, another
American textile manufacturing
firm, Belding-Heminway Co., was
creating a line of textile prints
called "Safari," designed by
illustrator Frederick Suhr (Dietz,
pers. corr. with author).[3] The
series was inspired by the book

Safari: A Saga of the African Blue
(1928) by Martin Johnson. Johnson
and his wife, Osa, went to East
Africa in the early 1920s where
they took enormous quantities of
photographs and film, returning
to the United States in 1927
after three years to travel the
Vaudeville circuit, and become
well-known explorers through their
films, writings, and lectures. The
Johnsons were Barnumesque in
their shameless self-promotion,
so it is fitting that they would
have had contact with the fashion
world.[4] The Johnsons are credited
with creating the idea of the "photo
safari."[5] Their work "made them
the most famous adventurers
(along with 'Bring 'Em Back
Alive' Frank Buck) in the world
of pop Africana" (Cameron
1990: 91).

Osa Johnson was given the
honor of choosing the names for
the Belding-Heminway prints. She
based the print subjects on four
African themes: Native, Animal,
Foliage and Flower, and African
Cities. She named the patterns
"Samburu, African war gear;
Utunda, circlets made of wild
animal teeth; Kando, jungle hunt
for leopard; Twiga, giraffe; Chui,
leopard; Simba, lion; Tinga-Tinga,
fronds of the palm tree; Tunda,
berries of the jungle; Chanua,
bloom; and Yamti, foliage"
(*American Silk Journal*, 1930b: 40).
American *Vogue* advertised the
line as "The New African Prints" in
January of 1930:

*Bright berries of the African
jungle are the theme of
"Tunda," this unique printed
crepe for the Spring ensemble.
Inspired by the exotic beauty of*

Africa, these new silks take their name from "safari," that journey into the jungle for big game a new adventure of the smart world. Safari prints for daytime and evening dresses, sports costumes and pajamas, are now displayed in the leading fashion shops. (1930: 16a)

Another Belding advertisement for the Safari line, "Silks of a New Adventure," included a zebra print called "Punda" (Figure 16). Note that the stripes are placed in a zebra abstracted into triangles. The print was used for a pajama pant designed by Schiaparelli, a logical choice as she was a universally recognized designer previously associated with the use of African motifs. The advertisement is a microcosm for everything that was appealing and modern about Africa—exotic tans, airplanes, and the savage jungle hunt:

To Africa ... the new playground ... The chic world goes for sun-bathing in Tunis, sport-flying over the Mountains of the Moon, journeying "On Safari," that jungle-hunt for fantastic game. And Africa, country of amazing contrast, savage and sophisticate ... this is the theme of Safari ... silks patterned in the keener color, the bolder rhythm of a new adventure. (Reproduced in Tortora and Eubank, 1989: 179, pl. 41)

The Safari Silks line of textiles was remarkable enough at the time for the Newark Museum in New Jersey to collect eleven samples. The print in Figure 17, probably named Samburu (African war gear) or Kando (jungle hunt for leopard) was made into a pair of pajama pants dating from the early 1930s found in The Ohio State University's Historic Clothing and Textiles Collection. The pants have a very wide leg with side panels in a solid-colored chartreuse-green silk crepe and waist ties. Because pajama pants were considered an exotic garment silhouette in 1930, they were appropriate for exotic textile subjects.

Several photographs from *Safari: A Saga of the African Blue* inspired the textile print in Figure 17. A man standing behind his shield suggests the positioning of the face behind the shield (Johnson 1928: 265). These Africans photographed were identified as Lumbwa warriors. The Lumbwa (Kipsigis) lived in what is now Tanzania in East Africa. In another photograph the half-circle shapes and zigzagged edges on a Lumbwa shield are very similar to those on the textile's shield (Ibid.). The shields were carried in battle (often cattle raids on other groups) and on lion hunts. The patterns on shields carried by the Masai, a neighboring group, were meant to identify individuals; therefore every shield was unique. They signified age group, geographic origin, lineage, military associations, and bravery as a warrior. Fashion also played a role in the design of Masai shields, as patterns changed over time according to the tastes of those who carried them (Plaschke and Zirngibl 1992: 36; Spring 1993: 122–3).

Western artists took advantage of the shield's perception as a symbol of the violence and savagery of African people by frequently utilizing shield patterns in textile prints and other fashionable objects. The representation of Africans in the Belding-Heminway textile would have been identified as an image of the "exotic primitive" by Sterling Brown (1937) in his work on the literary representation of Negroes by white authors, or as the "threatening subhuman" by Guy McElroy in his more recent work on the image of blacks in art (1990).[6] These stereotypes had a long history, thus the shield designs, embodying the fantasy of Africa, were a form of transformation of African art into modern aesthetics. Yet they illustrated modern ethics by retaining in subject matter untransformed and embedded negative stereotypes.

The image of the Masai shield was used consistently at the end of the 1920s and early 1930s. Variations were found in several textile sample books, including those issued by Arnold Print Works in 1929, which had a geometric print variation combining Zulu shield shapes and, strangely, hearts, available in three colorways: red, blue, and green. In 1932–3 Arnold was still exploring this motif print with a tiny red and white pattern of shields.[7] In the 1932 updated addition of her 1909 *Costume Design and Illustration*, Ethel Traphagen included a photograph of a student wearing a dress from a textile based on an African shield. Beside the photograph was an accompanying photograph of the shield that inspired the textile, carried by an African-American. Shields and African art motifs were also used for a cut velvet in a dress in the collection of the Museum at the Fashion Institute of Technology (accession number 74.43.1). The sleeve and skirt hems are trimmed in fur, adding to the "savage" theme of the fabric. The use of fur from African animals, prints based on fur patterns, and illustrations of animals indigenous to Africa, exoticized the natural world of Africa.

Images of African animals were more enduringly popular than any other African image (Hannel 2002). Illustrations of giraffes, lions, elephants, gazelles, and zebras accompanied most articles or travel advertisements related to Africa. The animals in Africa were a huge draw for people who had the financial means to travel there: "Mrs. Charles Minot Amory would rather go back to Africa than any place she has ever been—and she has been almost everywhere! Victoria Falls were very impressive, but the animals of Africa are what lure her to return" (*Vogue*,

Figure 16
Detail of Safari silk fabric "Punda" by Belding-Heminway Co., 1930. Newark Museum, New Jersey (30–33).

December 15, 1933: 25). Names of African animals were assigned to fabric colors, like "Lionness" for a gold-brown color (*The Fabric Guide, Spring 1927*: 56, 60, 62).

The novelty textiles of the 1920s and 1930s were quick to incorporate prints of African animals. Between 1925 and 1930 Poiret designed a fabric for the American firm of Schumacher called "Gazelles" (Helen Louise Allen Textile Collection, University of Wisconsin, Madison, (P.R. US 345). The brown and red gazelles placed between brown and tan zigzag patterns is yet one more example of the juxtaposition of the natural or primitive world with the geometry of the modern world. The American firm, Cheney, also printed a silk with leaping gazelles (*Vogue*, August 15, 1936: 76.).

Depictions of African animals were closely associated with colonial art. Raoul Dufy was a French watercolorist and textile designer who sought inspiration from many sources, including colonial themes. He created textiles patterned with whimsical African animals as well as images of the African landscape. He began his textile design career by creating dress fabrics for the couturier Paul Poiret in 1911. In 1912, Dufy became a textile designer for the Lyonaise silk textile firm, Bianchini-Férier, where he designed clothing and household fabrics until around 1928 (*Raoul Dufy* 1977). A dark pink silk and metal-thread fabric from 1923 called "L'Éléphant" from his Bestiaire collection of fabric for Bianchini-Férier is a rollicking example of his interest in African animals (Bowman 1985:

68). The elephant is probably an African elephant given the size of its ears in relation to its body (assuming the artist knew the difference between African and Indian elephants). The print also contains leopards and birds. The textile must have had some success because Poiret used "L'Elephant" for a medieval-inspired cloak or dress, probably from the same period. The textile was again illustrated in 1924 as a short, fur-trimmed coat in the *Gazette du Bon Ton* (July 1924–25: 361). Dufy repeated this theme of the elephant, bird, and leopard in a similar print on cotton called "La Jungle", *c.* 1924, which was reprinted in the 1950s (*The Art of Textiles* 1989: 159).

While images of African people were less frequent than images of African animals, interpretations of their appearance were printed onto many textiles, the warrior image illustrated in Figure 17 being a favorite stereotypical representation. Leon Bakst's textile print design in Figure 18 illustrates the most ubiquitous image of Africans during the Africana craze—the blackamoor (Hannel 2002). Bakst was born in Russia, trained in France, and known for his Orientalist costumes for Diaghilev and the Ballet Russes. He also designed textiles influenced by Persia, India, Peru, Crete, and Africa (Gibson 1929: 108–13). The textile was designed during his stay in the United States in 1923 and was exhibited by the Art Center in New York City five years after his death. Despite credit being given to a Kota funerary statue for inspiring Bakst's figures (Figure 19; *Design* 1930: 23), the upward,

Figure 17
Detail of a Safari silk "Kando" or "Samburu" by Belding-Heminway Co., 1930. Newark Museum, New Jersey (30–31).

carrying, position of their hands reminds one of the hand positions of blackamoors. The figures are black, their dress alternates from red to blue, and the color of crows alternates between greens and blues. "Nothing could be more brilliant. The color is barbaric in its intensity and suggests the cruelly bright contrasts of the tropics" (Gibson 1929: 112). The use of white around the eyes of the black figures and the presence of crows/blackbirds suggest racist stereotypes and images of blacks found in the United States. The darker color of the figures, and the use of bold lines and geometric shapes are the only qualities linking the textile to African-inspired themes.

The earliest use of the term blackamoor was during the sixteenth century when it was defined as "a black-skinned African, an Ethiopian, a Negro." The terminology has also been used to describe the color black and as a synonym for the devil (*The Oxford English Dictionary*, s.v. "blackamoor"). Blackamoor or "black slave" images were sculpted into candle stands, table legs, and torch bearers for stairways in eighteenth-century Venice, hence the term, "Venetian Blackamoors." Blackamoors were again popular during the Victorian period and in the twentieth century during the 1920s and to the end of the 1930s (*Vogue*, August 1, 1926).

The Bakst textile print illustrates how physical details in a design could be taken from influences perceived as African, and then transformed through the addition of Western stereotypes about Africans. While the blackamoor image had whimsical, fantastical aspects, as seen in Schiaparelli's fancy dress blackamoor costume worn to Le Bal Oriental in 1935 (Horst 1971), the blackamoor image is related to Brown's (1937) contented slave and McElroy's (1990) servile menial and, interpreted from current points of view on racism, has potentially negative associations with racial stereotyping, casting the role of an enslaved human being as either an exotic pet or decorative curio. In the United States a contented slave image was appealing because it harkened back to a mythical period in American history when African slaves were perceived to be happy and carefree.

Earlier versions of the blackamoor image may have had more positive associations (Valdes

Figure 18
Textile print with "Primitive African motifs" by Leon Bakst, ca. 1923–1924 (Gibson 1929: 113).

Figure 19
Kota funerary statue said to be the inspiration for Bakst textile in Figure 18. (Gibson 1929: 113).

y Cocom 2005). Blackamoor heads were occasionally part of European coats of arms. Initially thought to be trophies symbolizing victories over the Moors during the crusades, Valdes argues the blackamoor arose from several sources, including St Maurice and Prester John. St Maurice was an Ethiopian who has been the black patron saint of the Holy Roman Empire since the tenth century. Maurice and his Theban legion, comprised of thousands of Christian Africans, were called from

Africa to quell an uprising in Gaul. When they were ordered to give thanks to the Roman gods, they chose to be martyred rather than forsake their Christian faith. St Maurice was portrayed as a knight in full armor bearing a standard and a palm, and came to represent the universality of the Christian Church.

A second possible source for blackamoor images is Prester John, an Ethiopian emperor whose mythical status as a priest and king in a peaceful land was inspirational to twelfth-century European leaders torn by the conflicts of church and state. St Maurice and Prester John became linked because they were both "ideal soldiers in an ideal state" (Ibid.: 2). Because Prester John was descended from Solomon and thus had the blood of Christ, he was the only person permitted to bear as arms the image of the Crucifix. The earring worn by blackamoors is associated with this heraldic privilege. In the book of Leviticus, slaves who stayed with their masters after being freed underwent a ritual ear piercing. The title "Slaves of the Cross" was an important royal title in Ethiopia, thus the gold ring in a blackamoor's ear was a symbol of Christian devotion. Valdes believes that eighteenth-century blackamoor figures were meant to symbolize either injunctions or blessings.

The blackamoor image coincided with the rebirth of interest in North African and Orientalist themes in French fashion at the end of the 1930s. Despite the early 1920s date for the Bakst textile print, the rise in popularity of the blackamoor correlates with the decline of interest in jazz and primitive art themes in textiles, and, following the French in all things fashionable, the increasing Orientalism in the United States at the end of the 1930s (Hannel 2002).

Conclusion

By the second half of the 1930s as interest in Orientalist design was regaining momentum, the novelty of African themes in textiles was waning, as evidenced in a 1937 master's thesis titled, "Modern Design in Fabrics" (Dillman 1937), in which the only African influence listed was African-American jazz music. Dillman focused instead on cubist art and museum artifacts. Yet, African art was more visible than ever in popular fashion publications. A wooden Kota reliquary statue from Helena Rubenstein's apartment was given the same visual importance as a classical marble sculpture for a 1935 photographic backdrop (*Vogue*, April 1, 1935: 68–9). Schiaparelli's jewelry was photographed on a Gabonese sculpture (*Vogue*, October 15, 1938: 23). A Fang mask mirrored the face of a beautiful model for a *Vogue* cover (February 15, 1940), in turn mirroring Man Ray's now-famous 1926 photo *Blanc et Noir* (*Kiki*) of a white woman's face beside an African mask (*Paris Vogue*, May 1926: 37). During the 1930s African art went from being called "Negro" or "exotic" to "Modern art" (*Vogue*, November 15, 1933: 53; April 1, 1935: 69).

The creation of Africana textiles during the 1920s and 1930s was the result of increasing exposure to Africa through colonization, the visibility of African art and people exhibited at the many colonial and world expositions held between 1899 and 1939, interest in African art by European artists, and the presence of African-American performers dancing the cakewalk and the Charleston or playing ragtime and jazz in Paris, the cultural capital of Europe. As described in this article, African influence appeared in textiles at varying levels of borrowing. Copying or imitating African motifs led to quickly created products that were simultaneously seen as a way of improving Western art. Borrowing by adapting African geometric shapes like triangles or African rules of visual organization allowed artists some measure of creativity. In addition, these artists adapted the auditory feeling of jazz music into visual representations. Some textile artists sought different African sources, looking toward Western versions of Africa for their products. The source of inspiration was transformed from African motifs to long-held fantasies and racial stereotypes about Africa and its inhabitants.

Africana textiles satisfied aesthetic desires during the 1920s and 1930s. Geometric and abstracted shapes with strong graphic appeal through light and dark contrasts were attractive to urban populations because their patterns mimicked the hard lines and angles of skyscrapers, cars, and trains. While these designs reflected the technology of the period, they simultaneously satisfied desires to escape urban realities through their "primitive" origins. They were part of the pursuit of the exotic other and a simplified lifestyle as personified by the noble savage. The contradictory appeal of designs perceived as modern, primitive, and exotic reflected ambivalence during a period of cultural transition after the First World War. The visual rhythm and energy found in these fabrics also mimicked African-American music and dance, providing novelty demanded by consumers. By satisfying these desires, Africana textiles played a significant role in the development and promotion of Art Deco and modern design styles.

Notes

1. The term "Africana" was used throughout the period. Forstmann Fabrics advertised an "Africana" brown in 1930, one of three "midnight" browns (*Harper's Bazaar*, November 1930).

2. The Pahouin sculpture was photographed for both the exhibit catalogue (Sweeney 1935: 46), and by Walker Evans for a photographic portfolio created for educational purposes (Webb 2000: 13, 44).

3. Suhr is not mentioned in any of the primary documentation about the prints.

4. Osa also put her name onto a line of designer sportswear for women and children that used fabric trademarked, "Osafari." Colorways for the fabric were given names like Kedong Gold, Masai Bronze, Kenya Blue, Uganda Flame, Acacia, and Nandi. The clothing included shirts, slacks, shorts, jackets, and skirts, and had the label "Osa Johnson." Buttons for the line were wooden African masks (Imperato 1992: 207, 280, n. 7, 8). Osa also endorsed a "Congo" glove for the Spear glove company (*Vogue*, August 15, 1939: 46). In March of 1939 the Fashion Academy identified her as one of the twelve best-dressed women in America (Imperato 1992: 207).

5. Advertisements for travel to South Africa in American fashion magazines do not mention the "camera safari" until 1935 (see *Vogue*, September 1, 1935: 42).

6. Brown identified seven types of Negro characters represented by white authors in American literature: the contented slave, the wretched freeman, the comic Negro, the brute Negro, the tragic mulatto, the local color Negro, and the exotic primitive. McElroy identified four types of African-Americans in American art: grotesque buffoons, servile menials, comic entertainers, and threatening subhumans.

7. Both were to be produced in cotton. Textile books from Arnold Print Works, 3 July 1929 to 30 September 1929, 11 August 1932 to 30 January 1933, 60, American Textile History Museum Archives.

References

American Silk Journal. 1929. "Africa Symbolized in Silk Designs." March: 49.

—— 1930a. "Original Motifs in Spring Silks." January: 39–40, 49.

—— 1930b. "Safari Series by Belding-Heminway." 40.

—— 1931. "Barbaric Themes in New Season Silks." November: 40.

Archer-Straw, Petrine. 2000. *Negrophilia: Avant-Garde Paris and Black Culture in the 1920s*. London: Thames & Hudson.

The Art of Textiles. 1989. London: Spink & Son Ltd.

Barton, Oliver S. 1929. "African Baraza: An Incentive to Originality of Design." *American Silk Journal*: 48–9.

Benton, Charlotte, Tim Benton, and Ghislaine Wood (eds). 2003. *Art Deco 1910–1939*. London: V&A Publications.

Blake, Jody. 1999. *Le Tumulte Noir: Modernist Art and Popular Entertainment in Jazz-Age Paris, 1900–1930*. University Park: The Pennsylvania State University Press.

Bowman, Sara. 1985. *A Fashion for Extravagance: Art Deco Fabrics and Fashions*. London: Bell & Hymann.

Brown, Sterling Allen. 1937. *The Negro in American Fiction*. Washington, DC: The Associates in Negro Folk Education.

Buckberrough, Sherry. 1995. "Delaunay Design: Aesthetics, Immigration and the New Woman." *Art Journal* 52 (1): 51–5.

Cameron, Kenneth M. 1990. *Into Africa: The Story of the East African Safari*. London: Constable.

Chandler, Arthur. 1990. "Empire of the Republic: The *Exposition Colonial Internationale De Paris, 1931*." *Contemporary French Civilization* 14 (1): 89–99.

Clarke, Duncan. 1998. *African Hats and Jewelry*. London: PRC Publishing Ltd.

Coquet, Michèle. *Textiles Africains [African Textiles]*. Paris: Société nouvelle Adam Biro, 1998.

Crawford, M.D.C. 1916. "Bakuba's Contribution to Sports." *Women's Wear*, December.

—— 1917. "From African Soudan [*sic*] to Fifth Ave. Comes Gown Derived from Document." *Women's Wear* 15 (115): 5.

—— 1919. "The Designer and the Textile Industry." *The House Beautiful*, January: 16–17, 42.

—— 1923a. "Inspiration for Modiste Seen in Vogue of Congo Arts." *Women's Wear*, March 23: 31.

—— 1923b. "Textile Designs from Primitive Sources." Reprint from *The Lace and Embroidery* Review and Dress *Essentials*, May. Culin Archival Collection, General Correspondence. Brooklyn Museum of Art Archives, 1.4.051.

—— 1923c. "The Art of the Bushong Craftsmen." *Arts & Decoration*, June: 28, 29, 54, 60.

Culin, Stewart. 1923. Personal correspondence to Miss Hamburger, April 19. Culin Archival Collection, General Correspondence. Brooklyn Museum of Art Archives.

Damase, Jacques. 1991. *Sonia Delaunay: Fashion and Fabrics*. New York: Harry N. Abrams, Inc.

Deitz, Ulysses Grant. 1999. Curator of Decorative Arts, The Newark Museum. Personal communication with author, November 30.

de Meyer, Baron. 1930. "Baron de Meyer Views the Paris Collections." *Harper's Bazaar*, April: 61.

Design 1930. "Primitive African Number." 32(1).

Dillman, Martha Esther. 1937. "Modern Design in Fabrics." Unpublished Master's Thesis, Oklahoma Agricultural and Mechanical College.

Eicher, Joanne Bubolz. 1976. *Nigerian Handcrafted Textiles*. Ile-Ife, Nigeria: University of Ife Press.

The Fabric Guide, Spring 1927 [Cheney Brothers Silk Co., 1927], pp. 56, 60, 62. American Textile Museum Archives, Accession #1985.51.

Gazette du Bon Ton, 1924–5. "Au royaume du chatoiement" [To the glistening royalty]. July: 361.

Gibson, Katharine. 1929. "Textile Designs by Leon Bakst." *Design* 31 (6): 108–13.

Hannel, Susan L. 2002. The Africana Craze in the Jazz Age: A Comparison of French and American Fashion, 1920–1940." Unpublished Doctoral Thesis, The Ohio State University, Columbus.

Harper's Bazar ('*Bazaar*' after October 1929). 1922. "A Wrap and a Gown Vivid with the Color of the East." October: 46–7.

—— 1923a. "Embroidery Plays a Vital Part in the Paris Mode." April: 62–3.

—— 1923b. "Smart Women in Paris." September: 66.

—— 1926a. "A Modern Interior in Paris: Madame J. Suzanne Talbot's Residence." February 26: 54.

—— 1926b. "More Geometric Millinery from Agnès." July: 80.

—— 1928a. "Monsieur Lucien Lelong's Charming New Home in Paris." August: 64–5.

—— 1928b. "Vionnet Gown." November: 102.

——1928c. "Gay Sweaters for Winter Sports/Modernistic Designs Predominate." December: 80–81.

—— 1930. "Advertisement for Forstmann Fabrics." November.

—— 1935. "Mechanical Splendor—the Bolder the Better, the Crueler the More Chic." May: 94–5.

Herald, Jacquiline. 1991. *Fashions of the Decade: The 1920s*. New York: Facts on File.

Horst, Horst. P. 1971. *Salute to the Thirties*. New York: Viking Press.

Idiens, Dale, and K.G. Ponting. 1980. *Textiles of Africa*. Bath: The Pasold Research Fund Ltd.

Imperato, Pascal James and Eleanor M. Imperato. 1992. *They Married Adventure: The Wandering Lives of Martin and Osa Johnson*. New Brunswick: Rutgers University Press.

Johnson, Martin. 1928. *Safari: A Saga of the African Blue*. New York: G.P. Putnam's Sons.

McElroy, Guy C. 1990. *Facing History: The Black Image in American Art, 1710–1940*. San Francisco: Bedford Arts.

New York Times Magazine: 1923. "The World of Art: Two Museum Exhibitions." April 15: 12.

Paris Vogue. 1926. "Visage De Nacre Et Masque D'ébène [Mother-of-Pearl Face and Ebony Mask]." May: 37.

Picton, John, and John Mack. 1989. *African Textiles*. New York: Harper & Row.

Plaschke, Dieter, and Manfred A. Zirngibl. 1992. *Afrikanische Schilde: Graphische Kunstwerke Aus Dem Schwarzen Erdteil [African Shields: Graphic Art of the Black Continent]*. München: Panterra.

Poiret, Paul. 1927. "Will Skirts Disappear? A Thirty-Year Prophecy by the Paris Arbiter of Fashion." *The Forum* 77 (1): 30–40.

Raoul Dufy: Créator D'étoffes, 1910–1930 [Raoul Dufy: Fabric Creator, 1910–1930]. 1977. Paris: Modern Art Museum of the City of Paris.

Rhodes, Helen N. 1925. "Inspiration from the Congo." *Design* 27 (1): 1–4.

—— 1930a. "Analyzing the Primitive." *Design* 32 (1): 18–19.

—— 1930b. "Textile Inspired by Work of Primitive Peoples." *Design* 32 (1): 70.

Rubin, William. 1984. "Modernist Primitivism: An Introduction." In William Rubin (ed.) *"Primitivism" in 20th Century Art: Affinity of the Tribal and the Modern*, pp. 1–79. New York: The Museum of Modern Art.

Schiaparelli, Elsa. 1954. *Shocking Life*. New York: E.P. Dutton & Co., Inc.

Sheridan, Margaret. 1935. "Nomad at Home." *Vogue*, February 1: 52–3, 82, 84.

Spring, Christopher. 1993. *African Arms and Armor*. Washington, DC: Smithsonian Institution Press.

Stewart, van Campen. 1924. "Looking in at the Gate of the Dessert: A Description of a 'Terrifyingly Beautiful Land' and What a Paris Traveler Found Useful There." *Harper's Bazar*, March: 75–7, 134, 136, 138, 140, 142.

Stovall, Tyler. 1996. *Paris Noir: African Americans in the City of Light*. Boston: Houghton and Mifflin Company.

Sweeney, James Johnson (ed.) 1935. *African Negro Art*. New York: The Museum of Modern Art. (Reprint, 1966.)

Tortora, Phyllis, and Keith Eubank. 1989. *Survey of Historic Costume*. New York: Fairchild Publications.

Traphagen, Ethel. 1909. *Costume Design and Illustration*. New York: Brooklyn Public Library. (Reprint, New York: J. Wiley & Sons, 1932).

Valdes y Cocom, Mario. 2005. "Sigillum Secretum [Secret Seal]: On the Image of the Blackamoor in European History, Parts 1–3." Available online at: http://www. pbs.org/wgbh/pages/frontline/ shows/secret/famous/ssecretum1. html.

Vogue. 1926. "Advertisement for Mangone Coat and Dress Ensemble, New York." March 1: 104.

—— 1926. "Blackamoor: A Novel Decoration." August 1: 56–7, 94.

—— 1928. "Monsieur Lucien Lelong's Charming New Home in Paris." August: 64–5.

—— 1930. "Advertisement Safari Silks Line of Fabrics from Belding-Heminway." January 18: 16a.

—— 1931. "Captain Monyneux's Villa at Cap d'Ail." January 15: 66–7.

—— 1931. "Paris Parties Are Things of Beauty." October 15: 102.

—— 1932. "Shopping Hound's Tips on Christmas Gifts." December 1: 51.

—— 1933. "New Paris Apartment of Madame Helena Rubinstein." November 15: 52–3.

—— 1933. "Travel Trivia." December 15: 25.

—— 1935. (No title.) April 1: 68–9.

—— 1935. "Camera Safari-South Africa." September 1: 42.

—— 1936. "Gazelle Print." August 15: 76.

—— 1938. "Schiaparelli Jewelry." October 15: 23.

—— 1939. "The Congo Glove." August 15: 46.

Webb, Virginia-Lee. 2000. *Perfect Documents: Walker Evans and African Art, 1935*. New York: The Metropolitan Museum of Art.

White, Palmer. 1986. *Elsa Schiaparelli: Empress of Fashion*. London: Aurum Press.

Whitley, Lauren D. 1994. "Morris De Camp Crawford and American Textile Design, 1916–1921." Unpublished Master's Thesis, State University of New York, Fashion Institute of Technology.

Williams, Geoffrey. 1971. *African Designs from Traditional Sources*. New York: Dover Publications, Inc.

Women's Wear. 1923. "Cotton Frocks Shown by Bonwit Teller." April 14.

Wood, Ghislaine. 2003a. "Collecting and Constructing Africa." In C. Benton, T. Benton, and G. Woods (eds) *Art Deco 1910–1939*, pp. 78–89. London: V&A Publications.

—— 2003b. "The Exotic." In C. Benton, T. Benton, and G. Woods (eds) *Art Deco 1910–1939*, pp. 124–37. London: V&A Publications.

Hiding the (Fabric) Stash: Collecting, Hoarding, and Hiding Strategies of Contemporary US Quilters

Abstract

In this four-year, seventy-interview ethnographic study of US amateur quilters, I examine the guilty pleasures surrounding quilting practices, including the deviant acts of hiding both identity and fabric from family members and friends. While fabric is the medium of quilting, quilters purchase more than necessary for projects, slowly building up and hoarding a fabric stash. They then strategize hiding places for their fabric. Women's anxieties surrounding acquiring, hoarding, and hiding their fabric stashes highlight their diminished ability, relative to their spouses and their children, to pursue leisure activities without a stigma. Collecting and hiding the fabric stash become symbolic of women's attempts to carve out time ad space for themselves amid the multiple demands placed on them by such greedy institutions such as family and the workplace.

MARYBETH C. STALP

Marybeth C. Stalp is Assistant Professor of Sociology at the University of Northern Iowa. Her research is centered in gender, leisure and culture. In her quilting research she examines US midlife women's entrance into a traditional art form in contemporary times. Stalp also studies the emergence of Red Hat Societies, and amateur US cycling.

Textile, Volume 4, Issue 1, pp. 104–125
Reprints available directly from the Publishers.
Photocopying permitted by licence only.
© 2006 Berg. Printed in the United Kingdom.

Hiding the (Fabric) Stash: Collecting, Hoarding, and Hiding Strategies of Contemporary US Quilters

"Three of anything makes a collection." Anonymous

Introduction

People engage in the hobby of collecting for numerous reasons (Belk 2001). Some collectors display prized collections in living spaces (Csikszentmihalyi and Rochberg-Halton 1995), while others commemorate life events (Mavor 1997), or bond as a community of collectors, such as at Pez Dispenser collector conventions (Fogle 2002). Collecting and leisure activities share common ground, specifically in defending the time and space used to store materials to others not involved in the activity, including family members (Bartram 2001; Siegenthaler and O'Dell 2001). For example, dog sports competitors experience difficulty in negotiating boundaries between dog sports activities and paid-work demands (Gillespie, Leffler, and Lerner 2002); marathon runners and their spouses have sometimes conflicting perceptions regarding leisure time and family activities (Goff, Fick, and Oppliger 1997; Major 2001). Even romance readers (Brackett 2000; Radway 1991) and quilters (Abrahams and Pannabecker 2000; Doyle 1998; Gabbert 2000; Stalp Forthcoming) must engage in subterfuge to successfully enjoy their hobbies

under the radar of other family members.

Sometimes overlooked is the collector of utilitarian materials, such as "found art" collectors (Rothbart 2004; Zolberg and Cherbo 1997). Found-art collectors both collect and make use of their collections. They transform their collections (or part of their collections) into new and/or different forms, such as a collage. An example is the fabric collector who is also a quilter. A typical American quilter today is a middle-aged, middle- to upper-class woman who learns how to quilt as a hobby. She takes quilting classes, collects fabric, and makes use of her fabric collection for quilting (Stalp Forthcoming, 2001). Quilters collectively refer to their collections as "fabric stash," hoard fabric over time, and together strategize hiding places for the fabric stash in their homes. Collecting, hoarding, and hiding the fabric stash is a normal activity for quilters, and yet these acts are deviant to some, particularly those who share living space with them. Having a stash legitimates women's claims in identifying themselves as quilters and pursuing a leisure activity independent from the family institution. The presence of the fabric stash in the home also establishes the need for women's leisure space in the home. The meaning and role of the fabric stash in contemporary US women's lives is the central focus of this manuscript.[1]

I first bring the reader up-to-date on contemporary quilting practices, demonstrating how women can be understood as serious leisure quilters. I then review women's leisure pursuits in the home, conceptualize the traditional family as a greedy institution, one which promotes the deviant stigma of quilter. I next discuss the data and methods of the study, with the findings section following. The findings section explores how and why women collect, hoard, and hide fabric in the home. As women in this study engage in subterfuge to collect, hoard, and hide fabric from their families, they reveal the deviant stigma of quilter, the important gendered sites of negotiation for women and leisure in contemporary families, and provide evidence that modern families still operate as greedy institutions, influencing negatively women's leisure pursuits.

Quilting as Serious Leisure
In the US, quilting is a serious leisure activity that primarily women turn to for escape, relaxation, and creativity. Serious leisure is defined by Stebbins (1979: 3) as follows: "a systematic pursuit of an amateur, hobbyist, or volunteer activity that participants find so substantial and interesting that they launch themselves on a career, centred on acquiring

and expressing its special skills, knowledge, and experience." Most contemporary quilters in the US learn and practice quilting in serious leisure ways—they are not, for example, folk artists who learn to quilt primarily from family members (Becker 1982). Serious leisure quilters pay non-familial others for quilting instruction, learn to quilt as adults, and make quilts as individuals, rather than in the more historically familiar collective sewing circle, for example. And, although deeply involved in quilting activities, serious leisure quilters do not seek to have their work hanging in art museums as examples of high art. When quilting is practiced as a form of serious leisure, it is done so intensely, for individual pleasure, and it does not contribute directly to household monies. Quilting is aptly considered, as are other serious leisure activities, superfluous to the household economy.[2]

Mainstream stereotypical impressions of quilters focus on collective craft processes with pastoral images attached. Although quilters do continue to quilt in groups for charitable and/ or religiously affiliated projects, most contemporary quilters assemble quilts by themselves, on their own sewing machines and quilt frames, in their own living spaces. Serious leisure quilters gain emotionally, personally, and creatively from quilting, and they do not gain economically from it as this is not one of their goals. Women in this study engage in quilting because it helps them relax from paid work, unpaid household work, and other familial

duties, similar to other forms of serious leisure. Some women even use quilting activities to strengthen friendships in gendered ways by gifting quilts to family members and friends. A 2003 survey reports that the serious leisure quilter is a "dedicated quilter" who spends $1,556 annually on quilting materials, roughly a little over $100 a month (Leman Publications 2003).[3] Women in this study display similar tenets of expenditure, and range from middle to upper class. They pursue quilting for fun, not economic necessity or paid artistic pursuit.

Although women rarely gather to quilt collectively except for charitable events resembling an Amish quilting bee, for example, the positive collective aspects surrounding quilting activities still remain: devoted quilters gather regularly to discuss quilting, attend quilt shows, and shop for fabric and quilting materials. Rather than gathering around a quilt frame to complete a quilt together at quilting-related gatherings such as guild meetings, classes, and workshops, modern quilters instead learn as individual artists. Additionally, quilters use limited quilt guild meeting time to discuss issues relevant to the guild's status as a non-profit organization including annual fees, charitable events, organizing local quilt shows, and inviting quilt instructors from across the nation to teach specialized classes to the group.

Women's Leisure in the Home
Women have steadily entered the paid workforce since the 1970s, and family life has not

accommodated well to such changes, leaving women the double burden of paid work and the majority of the second shift of unpaid housework (Arrighi and Maume 2000; Crosby 1991; Greenstein 1996; Kluwer, Heesink, and van De Vliert 1997; Stier and Lewin-Epstein 2000). In addition, whereas men are believed to draw crisp boundaries between work and family activities, women have more fluid boundaries between public and private duties and the boundaries often blur or spillover, resulting in women having less control than men over their lives (Grzywacz and Marks 2000; Shaw 1998; Sirianni and Negrey 2000).

Stebbins (1996: 78) notes the particular, gendered challenges women barbershop singers face in order to practice their serious leisure:

Some women go to great lengths to ensure that basic family needs are met before they depart for a barbershop function ... they prepare in advance all the meals they will miss while away for a weekend convention or chapter retreat.

Women who pursue barbershop singing in serious leisure ways make choices in order to fulfill gendered expectations for their families, so that they can then engage in leisure pursuits. Similar to women barbershop singers and others engaged in serious leisure pursuits, quilters perceive that the time and space they devote to quilting can "take away" from their family's general needs, rather than help to meet them.

Not all leisure takes place outside the home, though, which can further complicate issues of time and space, as hobby activities and materials cannot be easily disguised. As Radway (1991: 103) indicates, women who read romance novels at home for leisure purposes feel guilty and rationalize their reading both to themselves and to their families: "They are aware that this activity demands the attention that would otherwise be devoted to children, house, or husband, but they defend themselves with the assertion that they have a right to escape just as others do." Issues of time and space surface as sites of family resource negotiation when women pay attention to themselves and engage in a serious leisure activity independent of the family, and one that occurs in the home in front of, or hidden from, family members.

Having a specific space set apart for creative needs has been important historically for men who pursue hobbies. Gelber (1999: 207) posits that the man's workshop emerged in the early 1900s in the US, and would be a place where men could "pursue messy craft hobbies without bothering their wives." Women may have been allocated the kitchen in the home, but it did not and still does not provide the type of leisure experience that men were seeking out at that time in a workshop (Doyle 1998). In contemporary middle-class homes in the US, if there is leisure space, men are more likely than women to have separate spaces for personal pursuits in the home such as a study, an office, or a workshop to pursue home-based leisure (Spain 1992).

Families, for men, provide more leisure than they do for women (Henderson, Hodges, and Kivel 2002; Mattingly and Bianchi 2003). Henderson, Bialeschki, Shaw, and Freysinger (1996: 39–40) point out that leisure for women (which could help relieve stress) gets squeezed out of women's daily lives and is not often legitimated:

Historically, almost all women have had to make leisure secondary in importance to the needs of the family. Family was an important component, both positive and negative, for women's leisure and continues today to exert great influence on women's lives, regardless of social class, race, or other life conditions.

When women do engage in leisure just for themselves, they typically find themselves negotiating their leisure activities with other responsibilities.

Women have less personal time, less private space, fewer economic resources, and less tolerance and respect than their male partners for pursuing the activities they enjoy and find fulfilling, especially leisure activities. Mattingly and Bianchi (2003: 1,014) note that "American men have more free time than women do, nearly half an hour more per day, on average." In addition, they suggest that "marriage has virtually no effect upon the free time of men but dramatically curtails that available to women" (Ibid.: 1,017). Even during family leisure activities such as holiday meals held in the home,

women often work while other family members rest, producing more leisure time for others than they do for themselves (Deem 1982; Di Leonardo 1987; Wearing 1998).

Families as Greedy Institutions
Sociologist Lewis Coser (1974: 6, 11) argues that the modern middle-class family best resembles a "greedy institution," one which makes unequal demands upon the wife-mother in comparison to the husband-father:

Greedy institutions are characterized by the fact that they exercise pressures on component individuals to weaken their ties, or not to form any ties, with other institutions or persons that might make claims that conflict with their own demands ... This patterned greediness, however, conflicts with other institutionalized arrangements in modern society and introduces instabilities and incongruities. These arise from incompatibilities between modern and traditional definitions of social roles.

Women in traditional heterosexual relationships are encouraged to strengthen ties within the family unit, and to weaken or eliminate ties with organizations that exist outside the family and may pull women away from expected family duties and roles. The greediness of the family structure pressures women to keep interests tied closely to family interests.[4]

Although Coser first wrote about families as greedy institutions in the early 1970s, more recent social

science research indicates that this phenomenon has unfortunately not dissipated for women in traditional heterosexual families. In contemporary society, traditional heterosexual married women have less free time than their husbands do on a daily basis (Green, Hebron, and Woodward 1987; Mattingly and Bianchi 2003), and women are still overwhelmingly burdened with the second shift of unpaid housework in addition to paid work responsibilities (Hochschild 1989). Therefore, as it consistently eats up women's leisure time, the institution of the traditional family can be successfully conceptualized as a greedy institution in relation to women's leisure opportunities.

When women attempt to carve out time for themselves for quilting, they feel guilt in doing so, and carry with them the stigma (Goffman 1963) of their serious leisure activity by hiding evidence of quilting (i.e., new fabric purchases) from family members (Stalp Forthcoming, 2001). Quilters, though not often thought to be on parallel with pot smokers, do have something in common with them—secrecy about their activities. Howard Becker (1963: 66–67), a sociologist, documents such secrecy practices involved in regular marijuana use, detailing that:

Although the user does not know what specifically to expect in the way of punishments, the outlines are clear: he fears repudiation by people whose respect and acceptance he requires both practically and emotionally. That is, he expects that his relationships with nonusers will be disturbed and disrupted if they should find out, and limits and controls his behavior to the degree that relationships with outsiders are important to him.

Women who quilt expect similar consequences from family members while participating in quilting—they expect that relationships with non-quilters (e.g., family members, friends, and co-workers) will be affected negatively should their quilting processes be revealed publicly, including collecting, hoarding, and hiding fabric. Note also that quilters make a marked effort to conceal their quilting identities from friends and co-workers who they believe will not be supportive. Additional gendered stigmas abound from friends and coworkers, including self-promotion, being old-fashioned, and fuddy-duddy.

Methods and Data

I used an ethnographic approach to collect data in which multiple sources and types of data were collected and included in the data set (Emerson, Fretz, and Shaw 1995). I conducted four years of participant observation, completed intensive unstructured interviews with seventy self-identified quilters—women who have developed or were in the process of developing a quilting identity—and used documentary photography techniques to capture visually the fabric stashes of participants. Purposive snowball sampling was used to contact these seventy participants, as well as to complete informal interviews with hundreds

of women quilters in the US. All participants are referred to in the text with pseudonyms.

The majority of interviews were tape recorded in person, and the remaining over the telephone. Guided by feminist methodology (Reinharz 1992), I used intensive unstructured interview techniques both to share voice and ownership, and to order conversation with participants. Extensive fieldnotes were taken within twenty-four hours of each interview and fieldwork experience (Lareau 1989), and I transcribed verbatim the majority of interviews. For those interviews hired out for transcription, interview tapes were reviewed while reading carefully through each transcript to ensure accurate transcription and comparable familiarity with each interview and transcript. After preparing transcripts, which ranged from twenty to fifty single-spaced pages, member checks were completed with participants and pseudonyms assigned to each participant to ensure confidentiality (Janesick 1994; Lincoln and Guba 1985).

The collection and analysis of data was consistent with the constant comparative method, simultaneously collecting and coding data, with emerging understandings and theoretical questions guiding further data analysis (Glaser and Strauss 1967). Analysis occurred by going back and forth between data collection, analysis, and writing, and I found the process to be beneficial in my understanding of the meaning of quilting to women. Even in the earliest stages of data collection I began to see that although these women lived in different parts of the country and that no two quilters were alike, they discussed similarly how they came to choose quilting as an activity, the process of becoming a quilter, as well as taking on the identity of a quilter.

Fabric Collecting

"I don't know why I love fabric, I just do." (Emily)

A quality collection of new 100% cotton fabric is an essential component of a quilter's life. A painter puts paint to canvas, a potter throws clay on a wheel, and a quilter creates quilts with fabric. Many quilters describe quilting as "a way of painting with fabric." In order to paint with fabric, quilters need access to and possession of a large variety of fabrics, many of the fabrics being new, rather than scraps of family clothing, for example. In this way, then, quilters are both creators of collectible objects (quilts), and collectors of objects (fabric).

Depending on quilters and their spaces, they arrange fabric in ways that best suit them: project, color, fabric type (e.g., solids, patterns, reproductions, hand-dyed, marbled, batiks). Regardless of how much money most quilters have, when able, they are willing to devote substantial resources to equipment. Quilters refer to their fabric collections as *fabric stash*, or *stash*. Many women with permanent quilting space in the home store their fabric in a cleaned-out clothes closet or utility closet somewhere in the home, and arrange fabric by color.

By arranging fabric in this way, quilters can easily see what their fabric palettes will provide them. They can then quickly assess which fabrics will work with any given project, or if they need to shop for new fabrics. Importantly, by having a fabric stash available in this way, quilters simply have to open the closet door to have immediate access to fabric. Those without permanent space rely upon plastic storage bins, cardboard boxes, or

plastic garbage bags to store their fabric. These women are not able to see their palette at a glance, and, in comparison to those with permanent quilting space, spend extra time sorting through fabric before beginning a project.

Note that in Figure 2 the boxes stashed in the closet are labeled—quilt fabric is in boxes with colors written on the boxes (e.g., Green and Yellow), while "Clothing Fabric" marks boxes that contain fashion fabrics. This woman's stash covers both sewing and quilting. Understandably, the concept of stash is not restricted to quilters, for other crafters such as weavers, knitters, and women who crochet also refer to their collection of raw materials necessary to their type of cultural production as stash (for popular press examples of quilting and knitting books, see Gervais 1995; Lydon 1997; Myers 2001; Ryer 1997; and Stoller 2004). The fabric stash represents important and revealing elements in quilters' lives. Fabric collections and the space they take up reveal

Figure 1
Visible Fabric Stash Arranged by Color.

Figure 2
Fabric Stash Hidden in Closet.

the primacy of women's identities as quilters within the home. Quilters with in-home access to quilting materials can make quilts continuously.

Women are quite attached to their fabric collections. In interviews with individual women, and in participant observation with quilters in small groups, women discuss the importance of a good fabric stash, joke with one another about how large their stashes are, and recommend ways of hiding fabric from family members. While conducting fieldwork at quilt shows and quilt guild meetings, as well as at individual interviews, women gave me suggestions about how to hide my fabric stash from a future spouse. Quilters advised me that when I finally settled down, I would need to learn how to hide my fabric stash from family and friends. In such jovial discussions, women often justified their fabric collections, or rationalized a fabric purchase (e.g., I know I will use this soon, which is why I bought so much of it). For example, in an interview setting with her husband in the next room, Meg justified her large fabric stash because she lives in the country, away from town and fabric stores:

The fabric stash is your palette.
See, I justify it [fabric stash]

because I live so far out. I can't just run down the street and get thread or get another piece of fabric. If I don't have it, it's an effort to get in the car and go for half an hour to get fabric. So I have a real justification for all my stash [laughter].

The presence of a fabric stash does not ensure that women are always able to find materials to work with for every project. Cassie has a fabric stash, but what fabric she has on hand does not always meet upcoming projects. This makes it necessary to go shopping for more quilt materials. She realizes that her husband views the stash differently than she, as he negatively refers to it as a "stockpile" rather than a stash. Before embarking on a new quilting project, she checks her stash to see if what she has will work: "I always out of guilt go to the stash first. I'll at least go through it before I look at a store to buy more fabric."

Quilters often engage in this somewhat jovial, somewhat serious line of fabric stash justification, and compare quilting to other activities, or habits: "Hey, I could be drinking, gambling, or smoking—quilting is much healthier." When criticized for their quilting activities, women are quick to make comparisons with other potentially addictive pursuits, demonstrating the harmlessness of quilting compared to the potential danger of activities in which they could otherwise be involved.

Fabric Hoarding

Women buying new fabric for quilting on a regular basis are at the mercy of the fabric market for what colors, patterns, styles, and designs are attainable and affordable. The majority of quilters purchase new 100% cotton fabric designed and printed specifically for quilting from readily available outlets: general fabric stores that also sell quilting fabric, quilt shops which specialize in quilting fabric, and websites. Fabric companies produce particular designs by season, and most stores have a limited supply of any given fabric. Dye lots and designs of quilt fabric change over time and in examining a quilter's fabric stash over a number of years, women are able to approximate in which decade a certain piece of fabric was produced—as with clothing, shoe, or automobile production, planned obsolescence also exists in the quilting world—fabrics from the 1970s may noticeably clash with fabrics from the late 1990s. Similar to how an artist might discuss raw materials in terms of need for future projects Denise describes how fabric fashion trends influence fabric selection in her quilting fabric purchases:

Figure 3
Bumper Sticker from Waechter's Silk Shop, Asheville, NC. Reprinted with permission of Waechter's Silk Shop, 2004. All rights reserved. Photograph taken by Pattiy Torno.

Lately I've been buying tans and browns and greens that I know I can't get in two or three years and I buy them now and then in two or three years, I'll use some of them for projects now, but in 2 or 3 years I'll have them in my stash. You buy what you know you will need in the future even if you know you don't need it right that second.

Perhaps due to this supply-controlled relationship between supply and demand, quilters admittedly overdo it when buying fabric for if they run out of a certain piece of fabric they cannot simply replace it with an identical piece: "When I see something I like, I buy a lot of it because I know if I don't, it will be gone when I come back to buy more." Quilters buy fabric for multiple reasons: for a specific project, it was on sale, or they need a particular color or type of fabric to add to their collections for future projects. Note in Figure 4 the sign in a quilt store window, not so subtly guiding quilters to purchase more fabric.

Sometimes, quilters are coaxed by an encouraging sign to buy fabric, and, sometimes, fabric just catches their eye and whispers to them in the store to bring it home. Acquiring fabric can be a gleeful experience, comparable to collecting rare cultural objects. For example, Beth describes her friend who became ecstatic about her fabric purchase:

My friend had ordered fabric from a national company through the mail and when her fabric came it was like GASP! I said she was having an orgasm just looking at the fabric! She said, "There are solids I have never seen!"

Women who quilt admittedly collect more fabric than they will probably ever use. Theresa realizes that she has a lot of quilting materials, evidenced by the amount of money she's

Figure 4
Sign in Quilt Shop to Buy More Fabric.
Photograph by Jane Wilson.

invested in quilting: "I have far too much money wrapped up into my quilting. But it's really been cheap entertainment." Although she feels she has gone a bit overboard on collecting quilting materials, Theresa implies that her positive quilting experience is harmless entertainment. Kelly discusses the role quilting plays in her life in similar ways: "Quilting has become quite an obsession that I wouldn't have expected it to be." As quilters strategize with one another about how to assemble and defend their fabric collections among the constraints of family life, as women at midlife, they are also concerned with what will happen to their carefully collected stashes if no family member takes a similar interest. Supportive of this notion is Figure 5, "The Quiltmaker's Will" that was hung in many women's quilting spaces, and was also referenced in multiple conversations with quilters.

Note that in "The Quiltmaker's Will" the explicit acknowledgement that non-quilters lack the proper understanding of a fabric collection: "_____hasn't the least appreciation for or for that matter knowledge of my extensive fabric collection—which collection is suitably deposited in sundry places for safe keeping." This lack of appreciation is also illustrated in the directives of the will, pointing the fabric inheritors to the most likely resting grounds of a misunderstood quilter's fabric stash: "... before the dumpster, search out my collection which is similarly stored. That said

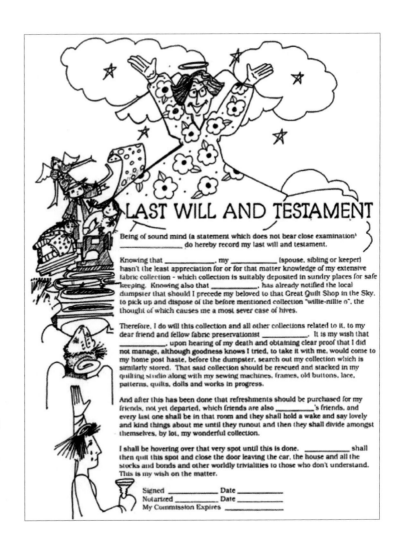

Figure 5
"The Quiltmaker's Will." Reprinted with permission of Elinor Peace Bailey.

collection should be rescued and stacked in my quilting studio"; and providing instruction of what is to happen to the fabric stash: "they shall divide amongst themselves, by lot, my wonderful collection."

Throughout countless interviews, women joked about how when they died their families would not know what to do with their fabric collections, and they were afraid their collections would get thrown away. This concerned them beyond joking about it, as many women had planned to open up their houses to quilting friends who could collectively determine what to do with the fabric, or put quilting friends in their wills so that they would have some control over what would happen to their valuable fabric stash. For example, Karla states,

> I don't know when I will ever get to use it all but as they say, "the one who dies with the most fabric wins" and I have a will in there on the wall that when I pass away my husband is to call five or six different people and they are to come at once, not to buy but to take fabric. They can just have whatever is in there.

Fabric hoarding practices, such as Karla's, result in a long-term overabundance of fabric. What to do with one's fabric stash is something many aging quilters are contemplating. They want the fabric to go to someone who will appreciate it, and will cherish it as they have over time. Similar to family heirlooms, the fabric stash carries sentimentality with it.

Fabric Hiding

"It's amazing what you do to hide fabric." (Melinda)

Women often strategize with other quilters to deceive family members about the costs of their quilting activities. They distort information about the amount of money they spend on fabric and other quilting materials and the accumulated fabric stash they have already purchased. Interestingly, women also hide their fabric stash from family members, and assist each other in devising ways to keep fabric hidden from others.

One legendary tale was passed on in a group interview where the women were sharing their "stash stories." These women worked together at a fabric store in the western US, and were remembering their more colorful customers. Tracy shared that "one woman took all of the food out of her freezer and lined the freezer bottom with fabric and put the food on top so her husband never knew." While discussing this fabric stash-hiding genius, the women seemed somewhat conflicted. They admired her for finding such a good hiding place, but were also saddened by the deceit they practice in order to continue to quilt.

As the conversation progressed, Carrie recounted her own dilemma about having to hide new fabric purchases from her family. Since Carrie works at a fabric store, she is perpetually tempted by fabric. She came home after working late one night and unexpectedly encountered her still-awake husband. Faced with exposing her most recent fabric stash purchase to him, Carrie thought quickly to hide her newest fabric purchase:

I brought home a big bag of fabric and I'm thinking, he's usually asleep. I come in and he's awake, and I have this huge bag. And I remember opening the door and I said, "Oh, you're up." I dropped the bag, so it's sitting out on the front porch, under the mailbox. So I'm thinking I'll just get it when he goes to bed. We'll watch Friends and we'll go to sleep, or he'll go to sleep. Well, he ran outside to the van to go get whatever, his planner or something and he comes back in and he says, "Did you forget something?" I went, "Oh." And he just put it on the couch and shook his head and said, "Good Night." That was the last time I hid fabric. I was so embarrassed because he caught me. He caught me.

This passage proves particularly interesting, as Carrie documents that it is through the family framework that she feels limits and she then passes judgment on her own serious leisure activities. Cassie's statement, "I was so embarrassed because he caught me. He caught me," indicates her guilt and feeling that she should not perhaps be participating in an activity that must be kept hidden from her family. In this way, then, quilters do to some extent feel that their activities are deviant to normal family activities, carry a stigma with them concerning their quilting, and choose to keep it a

hidden activity from family and friends.

Since this event, Carrie no longer hides fabric from her family. Yet, despite her attempts to make more public her interest in quilting (and therefore trying to legitimate and normalize the activity for her family), her extended family continues to tease her about her fabric stash and quilting in ways that make her uncomfortable:

I have a section of the basement now. I took up the dining room for about four years and I was really embarrassed the other day. My sister-in-law said, "When did you buy that?" referring to the dining room table, and I said, "Four years ago." It was embarrassing. I said, "Didn't you know that's what my fabric sat on?" I mean, they knew my fabric was sitting on there, why couldn't they figure it was sitting on something? My father-in-law said, "Hey, you moved your stuff." I said, "Yes." I didn't know it was so big.

Carrie used to keep her quilting materials on the dining room table as a temporary quilting space. When she was finally able to move her materials to a permanent quilting space in the basement, her extended family noticed, leaving her with feelings of embarrassment. She was embarrassed for reasons other than quilting, though. Her passion for quilting had revealed the neglect of keeping the house up to her in-laws' standards. Therefore, Carrie felt that perhaps her in-laws were not simply commenting on

her fabric stash, but that her fabric stash was getting in the way of her other wifely duties, like keeping a clean house and entertaining guests with regular use of the dining-room table.

Similarly, Melinda, who also works at a fabric store, remembers the first time she hid fabric from her family:

I read a book about fabric-aholics and I thought, "Oh, I'm getting to that point." One day I worked an evening shift, I left some of my fabric in the car, in the back of the car, and I thought, "Oh, I'll just get it tomorrow, my husband will be gone." I think he had the day off and I'm thinking, "Oh, this plan is not working because now he's going to see me bringing it in during the day." It's amazing what you do just to hide fabric.

When Melinda and other quilters discussed their hiding strategies, they indicated the extent to which they were attached to their fabric purchases and quilting practices. Continuously hiding fabric also reveals the household tensions concerning women's abilities to engage in quilting in open, common family spaces.

Loretta, for example, hides her fabric in similar ways to Carrie and Melinda, although she states that her husband and family are fully supportive of her quilting:

I have fabric in the trunk of my car, and it's so dumb, my husband does not care. I'll go buy stuff and leave it in the trunk, and after everybody goes to sleep I'll go get it and take it

*in the house. Now why? They
don't care. It's just like you know
that you're obsessed, so I guess
it's like a bulimic person, you
don't want anybody to know that
you're eating, although they
know you are, so you sneak it
and you hide it, and then when
it gets melted in there with
everything else nobody knows.*

*Int: Does it have anything to do
with the fact that it's yours, it's
just yours?*

*Yeah. And it's just mine,
because when you're raising
a family, you are doing
for everybody else and
making quilts gives you an
accomplishment.*

The link Loretta makes between
her enjoyment in quilting and
family constraints that limit her
time doing it prove revealing, and
support the notion of families as
greedy institutions. Additionally,
Loretta likens her quilting activities
to the eating disorder of bulimia
in terms of hiding and hoarding
her fabric, stating that she knows
she is obsessed with fabric, and
is choosing not to reveal her
obsession to her family. Although
Loretta indicates that she has
support from her family for her
quilting activities, she still feels the
need to guard this part of her life
from the non-quilters in her family,
as if she were hiding a stigmatized
addiction.

Cultural Contradictions of Quilting

Viewing quilting from women's
perspectives highlights not just
the relevance of quilting in lives
of individual women, but also

the ways in which women feel
constrained in pursuing quilting in
the home. Although women in this
study are living quite traditional
lives and are using finished quilts
in traditional family-linked ways
(e.g., bed coverings, small wall
hangings, and gifts for family and
friends), the process of quilting
comes into question as it takes up
women's attention and time, as
well as space in the home for the
fabric stash. Quilting along with
other specialized and compelling
activities (e.g., hunting, fishing,
golfing) are individually pursued
processes that are often easily
misunderstood by outsiders.
Quilters in this study do perceive
outsiders to be dismissive, even
explicitly negative, toward their
passion for quilting. Angela
describes the encompassing
position that quilting currently has
in her life, and recalls how others
respond to her passion:

*People ask me, "What do you
do now that you are retired?"
I tell them, "I quilt." And they
look at me like, "Well, you
can't possibly spend all your
time quilting." They have no
conception that you really could.
No, you are not sitting in a chair
putting a needle in and out of
fabric all the time, but there
are so many aspects involved
in quilting that you literally can
spend your entire life totally
engrossed in quilting and I am
awfully close to doing that.*

The positive elements quilting
possesses, however meaningful
to those who do it, are not part
of mainstream society's general
knowledge of quilting specifically,

or of women's activities generally. Kelly, a quilter and an academic in her forties, struggles with being understood by outsiders. She is aware of the negative connotations attached to both aspects of her identity as a quilter and as a Ph.D. candidate. Her family has traditional notions of what women should be:

Nobody knows what academia is, nobody knows what a Ph.D. is. I don't have kids. If I had kids that would be part of the traditional American life that people understand. I really do think that this is a way that people understand me in a way that they don't understand other parts of my life.

Kelly is quite aware of the gendered family expectations present, as well as the quilting and feminine stereotypes that outsiders to quilting present to her: "I think it is really odd in a way but it kind of makes me think maybe I shouldn't quilt because I don't want to be pigeonholed in that way." Despite the paradoxes present in her work and her quilting life, Kelly continues quilting.

Cassie, a young professional in her early thirties, is careful with whom she shares her quilting interests in the workplace. Her reasons for guarding her quilting identity are similar to Kelly's. Cassie's colleagues certainly appreciate the workmanship present in finished products, yet they are openly suspicious and even hostile about the time she spends conducting such workmanship. They accept the finished quilts as valuable

cultural objects, and some of her co-workers have even hired her to make quilts for them, but the time and effort she has spent on them is what they question and judge negatively. For these reasons, Cassie is particularly cautious about sharing her quilting interests with outsiders: "I need to be careful of the people that I show my things to." She explains how people at work react to her as a quilter when she reveals her finished quilt products:

I don't want them to say, "Oh god, I don't do anything, you must do everything." That's not the image. So I try to make sure it's someone who's not going to say, "Well, when do you have the time? You work just as hard as we do!" I brought in a quilt that I had made and showed a couple of people and they did say, "Well, how can you do that?" It's a patronizing kind of remark, "Well, how do you do that and everything else?" So then I'm justifying it, because here I am not trying to self promote and then it seems like I'm self promoting, so I say, "Well, I don't have kids and I really don't have any hobbies besides running and so this is what I do to relax," which is all true. But I'm justifying why I'm doing something like this. I try to minimize it, but it does kind of get that response. I think more from the men it's, "Oh, you quilt" meaning kind of old-fashioned, or fuddy-duddy.

Interestingly, the excerpt from Cassie's interview demonstrates

the multiple standards for contemporary women. Her co-workers' knowledge of her quilting interests brings to light that Cassie feels she cannot be too successful in her quilting endeavors, or have too many time-consuming activities beyond paid work (not including children). The final insinuation by male co-workers that Cassie might be a fuddy-duddy because of her quilting, even causes her to be conscious of the potentially negative nature of her outside-work interests. They, similar to family and friends, appreciate the quilt as a finished product, but not the quilter as she engages in the actual process. Logically, without the quilting process, one would not have a quilt as a finished piece. To have a finished quilt, someone has to make it.

As evidenced in the data presented, these women value quilting on many important levels, yet they do not expect non-quilters to be interested in it, or value, quilting in the same ways that they do. Because of this, some quilters thought it unusual that I as a researcher would want to interview them about quilting. Many women claimed it was difficult to articulate in a way that would make sense to non-quilters why they quilted. Some women have been quilting for so long that it has become a fundamental part of their lives, evidenced in the intensity with which they talked about quilting as a passion. Others had never been asked, respectfully, about what quilting meant to them. While non-quilters who admire quilts often focus solely or primarily on the product—the finished quilt—quilters give far more emphasis to the process of quilting. To a quilter, *how* a quilt is produced is often as important, or even more important, than the finished quilt itself.

The language quilters use to describe and defend their serious leisure activities indicates that the family is a greedy institution for the women in this study. For example, the definition of a fabric collection as a "stash" links the fabric and the activity of quilting to other deviant or marginalized activities. The deviance women feel while participating in leisure is further evidence of their limited options to pursue leisure. As members of traditional families, women quilters in trying to pursue quilting, reveal the greediness of families, for families not only limit women's leisure pursuits, but family members also question the value of the activity. Carrie, who was caught hiding fabric from her husband and whose in-laws teased her about her fabric stash taking up the dining room table, has this to say about living with the stigma of quilting:

Why is there such a stigma on women? I mean, it's because of women that people are here, period. I mean, we bear children, we mother children, and men couldn't do what they do without us. I'm just like, give us credit, we work our butts off, and I am probably the most lax, lazy mom that I can think of, but if it wasn't for me, my kids wouldn't be who they are, my husband wouldn't be the way he is. It's because of women. And, okay, so we happen to enjoy getting together to spend an afternoon talking about quilts,

what's so wrong about that? My husband spent a whole day last weekend hunting a bird.

Carrie's frustration with the deviant label is clearly present in this excerpt. She both recognizes the stigma of quilting as perceived by her husband, and the myriad of other contributions she makes to the family, and has difficulty understanding "what's so wrong about that?"

Discussion

Contemporary quilting practices reveal much about women's leisure opportunities. There is overlap between fabric collecting and the leisure activity of quilting. Quilters collect fabric, but they also make quilts, using fabric from their collections. Women quilters collect to establish a fabric stash, a base from which to properly engage in their serious leisure activity. Similar to artists, quilters need a set of raw materials from which to draw. And yet, similar to other collectors, quilters are attached emotionally to their fabric stashes, and are not willing to cut some of it up for quilting.

The fabric hoarding of women quilters comes into question when their families challenge the need to have so much fabric collected that is not being used up to make quilts. One woman shared a discussion she had with her husband when he questioned why she kept accumulating fabric and did not ever seem to use any of the fabric stash up: "I said to him, 'This is my hobby. I collect fabric. Would you ask a stamp collector to mail a valuable stamp?'" This questioning process reveals the unique situation quilters are in as both collectors and participants of a serious leisure activity.

Hiding the fabric stash reveals how quilters perceive the lack of support from outsiders, family, and friends. Quilters feel that they must squeeze in their leisure practices among other everyday familial duties. Akin to illicit drug users, quilters engage in secret practices such as hoarding and hiding fabric to keep from their families the extent to which they are engaged in this activity. As they feel pressured to place quilting last in a day's scheduled events, quilters feel that their families do the same thing—place them last in a list of valued daily items. Convinced of non-support while alive, they also predict that their families will disrespect their fabric once they pass on. Simply hiding the stash is no longer the answer. Instead, women make arrangements with other quilters who value the years devoted to the fabric collection stored in the house, as evidenced with "The Quilter's Will."

Quilters in this study collect fabric and underreport both the amount of fabric purchased and related cost to family members, which is similar to others engaged in serious leisure pursuits. They also hoard fabric because it is a limited commodity, produced in specific amounts and guided by fashion cycles. Finally, women quilters hide their fabric stash from family members, and are not willing to divulge the vastness of their collections to non-quilting outsiders. Thus, the greedy institution of the family provides a framework through which to understand the development of deviant stigma surrounding women's leisure, and further promotes the deviance of the hidden activities involved in fabric collecting, hoarding, and hiding.

Women's leisure pursuits are typically ranked last both by family members and quilters themselves. By examining women whose leisure pursuits have risen up the leisure ladder of importance, we can also see the struggles women confront as they continue to quilt and continue to participate as active members of the families. Women carry the deviant stigma of quilter as they engage in subterfuge to collect, hoard, and hide fabric. Because in contemporary life quilting is not a necessity (and indeed may be a luxury), it is not always legitimated as an activity worthy of time, space, and resources, as other well-documented, non-utilitarian collectors and hobbyists experience. Thus, contemporary women performing a traditionally feminized needlework craft sometimes have to struggle and engage in subterfuge to do so successfully. That women are less free to use family resources to pursue traditionally feminized activities such as quilting reveals the still gendered configuration of home and family life, and contributes to the understanding of collectors and collecting in contemporary society.

I thankfully acknowledge Lori Seawel, Oksana Grybovich, Pattiy Torno, and Jane Wilson for their technological and photographic assistance.

Notes

1. An earlier version of this paper was presented at the International Quilt Study Biennial Symposium on Collecting, University of Nebraska, Lincoln, February 24–6, 2005.

2. Certainly, women and men do engage in quilting activities for capital. The women in this study, however, engage in quilting as a form of *non-economic* cultural production (Bourdieu 1993).

3. Note that an economical comparison to a masculine activity is similar. The US Fish and Wildlife Service reports that in 1996 of the 14 million hunters in the United States, the average hunter spent $1,475 annually on hunting expenditures (Hunting Statistics and Economics 2004).

4. In extreme situations, such as domestic abuse, the family can be understood not simply as a greedy institution, but as a total institution (Avni 1991; Goffman 1961). The women in this study, certainly, are not in this situation. This study is not an attempt to diminish cases of domestic violence or other instances of oppressive family situations.

References

Abrahams, Ethel Ewert, and Rachel K. Pannabecker. 2000. "'Better Choose Me': Addictions to Tobacco, Collecting, and Quilting, 1880–1920." *Uncoverings*: 79–104.

Arrighi, B.A., and D.J. Maume, Jr. 2000. "Workplace Subordination and Men's Avoidance of Housework." *Journal of Family Issues* 21(4): 464–87.

Avni, Noga. 1991. "Battered Wives: The Home as a Total Institution." *Violence and Victims* 6(2): 137–49.

Bartram, Sherry A. 2001. "Serious Leisure Careers Among Whitewater Kayakers: A Feminist Perspective." *World Leisure* 2: 4–11.

Becker, Howard. 1963. *Outsiders: Studies in the Sociology of Deviance*. New York: The Free Press.

— 1982. *Art Worlds*. Berkeley, CA: University of California Press.

Belk, Russell W. 2001. *Collecting in a Consumer Society*. London: Routledge.

Bourdieu, Pierre. 1993. *The Field of Cultural Production*. New York: Columbia University Press.

Brackett, Kim Pettigrew. 2000. "Facework Strategies among Romance Fiction Readers." *The Social Science Journal* 37(3): 347–60.

Coser, Lewis. 1974. *Greedy Institutions: Patterns of Undivided Commitment*. New York: The Free Press.

Crosby, Faye J. 1991. *Juggling: The Unexpected Advantages of Balancing Career and Home for Women and Their Families*. New York: The Free Press.

Csikszentmihalyi, Mihaly, and Eugene Rochberg-Halton. 1995. *The Meaning of Things: Domestic Symbols and the Self*. Cambridge: Cambridge University Press.

Deem, Rosemary. 1982. "Women, Leisure, and Inequality." *Leisure Studies* 1: 29–46.

Di Leonardo, Micaela. 1987. "The Female World of Cards and Holidays: Women, Families, and the Work of Kinship." *Signs* 12(3): 440–53.

Doyle, Amanda. 1998. "The Fabric of Their Lives: Quilters Negotiating Time and Space." *Women's Studies Journal* 14(1): 107–29.

Emerson, Robert M., Rachel I. Fretz, and Linda L. Shaw. 1995. *Writing Ethnographic Fieldnotes*. Chicago, IL: The University of Chicago Press.

Fogle, Melinda. 2002. "Joining the Pezzimist Party: Pez Convention as Rite of Passage and Communal Bonding." *Journal of Popular Culture* 36(2): 236–49.

Gabbert, Lisa. 2000. "'Petting the Fabric': Medium and the Creative Process." *Uncoverings*: 137–53.

Gelber, Steven M. 1999. *Hobbies: Leisure and the Culture of Work in America*. New York: Columbia University Press.

Gervais, Sandy. 1995. *Living the Life of a Fabric-aholic*. Algona, IA: Midlife Printing.

Gillespie, Dair L., Ann Leffler, and Elinor Lerner. 2002. "If it Weren't for My Hobby, I'd Have a Life: Dog Sports, Serious Leisure, and Boundary Negotiations." *Leisure Studies* 21: 285–304.

Glaser, Barney G., and Anselm L. Strauss. 1967. *The Discovery of Grounded Theory*. New York: Aldine de Gruyter.

Goff, Stephen J., Daniel S. Fick, and Robert A. Oppliger. 1997. "The Moderating Effect of Spouse Support on the Relation Between Serious Leisure and Spouses' Perceived Leisure-Family Conflict." *Journal of Leisure Research* 29(1): 47–60.

Goffman, Erving. 1961. *Asylums: Essays on the Social Situation of Mental Patients and Other Inmates.* Garden City, NY: Anchor Books.

—— 1963. *Stigma: Notes on the Management of Spoiled Identity.* Englewood Cliffs, NJ: Prentice-Hall, Inc.

Green, Eileen, Sandra Hebron, and Diana Woodward. 1987. "Women, Leisure, and Social Control." In Jalna Hanmer and Mary Maynard (eds) *Women, Violence and Social Control*, pp. 75–92. Atlantic Highlands, NJ: Humanities Press International, Inc.

Greenstein, Theodore N. 1996. "Husbands' Participation in Domestic Labor: Interactive Effects of Wives' and Husbands' Gender Ideologies." *Journal of Marriage and Family* 58: 585–95.

Grzywacz, Joseph G., and Nadine F. Marks. 2000. "Family, Work, Work-Family Spillover, and Problem Drinking During Midlife." *Journal of Marriage and Family* 62: 336–48.

Henderson, Karla A., M. Deborah Bialeschki, Susan M. Shaw, and Valeria J. Freysinger. 1996. *Both Gains and Gaps: Feminist Perspectives on Women's Leisure.* State College, PA: Venture Publishing, Inc.

Henderson, Karla A., Sonja Hodges, and Beth D. Kivel. 2002.

"Context and Dialogue in Research on Women and Leisure." *Journal of Leisure Research* 34(3): 253–71.

Hochschild, Arlie Russell. 1989. *The Second Shift.* New York: Avon Books.

"Hunting Statistics and Economics." 4/5/2004. US Fish and Wildlife Services. Available online at: http://hunting.fws. gov/huntstat.html.

Janesick, Valerie. 1994. "The Dance of Qualitative Research Design: Metaphor, Methodolatry, and Meaning." In Norman K. Denzin and Yvonne S. Lincoln *Handbook of Qualitative Research*, pp. 209–19. Thousand Oaks, CA: Sage.

Kluwer, Esther S., Jose A.M. Heesink, and Evert van De Vliert. 1997. "The Marital Dynamics of Conflict over the Division of Labor." *Journal of Marriage and the Family* 59: 635–53.

Lareau, Annette. 1989. *Home Advantage.* London: The Falmer Press.

Leman Publications, Inc. 2003. *Quilting in America Survey.* Golden, CO.

Lincoln, Yvonne S., and E.G. Guba. 1985. *Naturalistic Inquiry.* Beverly Hills, CA: Sage.

Lydon, Susan Gordon. 1997. *The Knitting Sutra: Craft as a Spiritual Practice.* New York: Harper Collins.

Major, Wayne F. 2001. "The Benefits and Costs of Serious Running." *World Leisure* 2: 12–25.

Mattingly, Marybeth, and Suzanne M. Bianchi. 2003. "Gender

Differences in the Quantity and Quality of Free Time: The U.S. Experience." *Social Forces* 81(3): 999–1,031.

Mavor, Carol. 1997. "Collecting Loss." *Cultural Studies* 11(1): 111–37.

Myers, Lisa R. 2001. *The Joy of Knitting: Texture, Color, Design, and the Global Knitting Circle.* Philadelphia, PA: Running Press.

Radway, Janice. 1991. *Reading the Romance: Women, Patriarchy, and Popular Literature.* Chapel Hill, NC: The University of North Carolina Press.

Reinharz, Shulamit. 1992. *Feminist Methods in Social Research.* New York: Oxford University Press.

Rothbart, Davy. 2004. *Found: The Best Lost, Tossed, and Forgotten Items From Around the World.* New York: Simon & Schuster.

Ryer, John. 1997. *A Husband's Guide to Quilt Appreciation.* Ventura, CA: Calico Press.

Shaw, Jenny. 1998. "'Feeling a List Coming On': Gender and the Pace of Life." *Time & Society* 7(2): 383–96.

Siegenthaler, Kim L., and Irma O'Dell. 2001. "Older Golfers: Serious Leisure and Successful Aging." *World Leisure* 1: 47–54.

Sirianni, Carmen, and Cynthia Negrey. 2000. "Working Time as Gendered Time." *Feminist Economics* 6(1): 59–76.

Spain, Daphne. 1992. *Gendered Spaces.* Chapel Hill, NC: University of North Carolina Press.

Stalp, M.C.. 2001. "Women, Quilting, and Cultural Production: The Preservation of Self in Everyday Life." Unpublished Dissertation, Athens, GA: University of Georgia.

—— Forthcoming. "Negotiating Time and Space for Serious Leisure: Quilting in the Modern U.S. Home." *Journal of Leisure Research*.

Stebbins, Robert A. 1979. *Amateurs: On The Margin Between Work and Leisure*. Beverly Hills, CA: Sage.

—— 1996. *The Barbershop Singer: Inside the Social World of a Musical Hobby*. Toronto, Ontario: University of Toronto Press.

Stier, Haya, and Noah Lewin-Epstein. 2000. "Women's Part-Time Employment and Gender Inequality in the Family." *Journal of Family Issues* 21(3): 390–410.

Stoller, Debbie. 2004. *Stitch 'N Bitch Nation*. New York: Workman Publishing Company.

Wearing, Betsy. 1998. *Leisure and Feminist Theory*. Thousand Oaks, CA: Sage.

Zolberg, Vera L., and Joni Maya Cherbo (eds). 1997. *Outsider Art: Contesting Boundaries in Contemporary Culture*. Cambridge: Cambridge University Press.

Book Reviews

Book Review

Knitwear in Fashion, Sandy Black (Thames and Hudson, 2005)

Here's the paperback edition of a book first published in 2002 and the publisher deserves a round of applause for making this handsome and useful book more available and affordable. Sandy Black is an experienced creative designer in her own right, always in touch—even in love—with her subject. She describes her book as an anthology, so it is selective, but it offers a broad picture. The author provides an intelligently integrated view of knitting and knitwear by showing clear links between materials, processes, structures and techniques and the design and style of an end product. Characteristically, the book explores the universality of knitwear in the light of the seemingly endless versatility and scope of knitted construction. The focus is on the twentieth and twenty-first centuries, particularly the last twenty five years.

The book may have a rather anodyne title but that belies the riches within. The "fashion" in its title makes its presence felt throughout the book and lends a gloss to it all. It is a generous size at A4, with page design that gets the best from a veritable cornucopia of color photographs. Some 285 color photographs definitely give it a "wow factor"

and also serve the author's text well. In a design-sensitive publication, it would have been good to acknowledge the book designer. Whoever they are, they succeeded in making this book a pleasure to use, an enticing page-turner for anyone with an interest in this absorbing field.

It's crisply written and well organized into three main sections. In order, they are: *Knitwear in Fashion—Fashion in Knitwear* with subsections *Re-inventing the Classics, Decades of Change* and *Creative Fashion Accessories*; *Innovation and Experiment-Making the Future* with sub-sections *Materials, Structures and Processes, Radical Knitwear* and *The Seamless Revolution*; *Blurring the Boundaries—Contemporary Art and Design* with sub-sections *Artworks and Sculptural Form, Knitwear in Performance and Design for Interiors*. Hiding at the back, behind another anodyne heading *Information*, comes one of the book's special contributions—illustrated sections on technologies, design yarns and fibers, eight useful pages of designer biographies, a bibliography and a technical glossary. There's also an index.

The origins of the book lie in the diversity of knitting,

Textile, Volume 4, Issue 1, pp. 126–129
Reprints available directly from the Publishers.
Photocopying permitted by licence only.
© 2006 Berg. Printed in the United Kingdom.

REVIEWED BY BARBARA BURMAN

precisely its attraction. These are best described in the author's own words. "It is this diversity that has led me to present this anthology of knitwear and knitting, together with a love of materials and construction, and a desire to celebrate this 'little understood' technique for its unique capabilities: the way in which it can engineer both two- and three-dimensional shape; its affinity with the body through innate characteristics of stretch-to-fit; and its infinite structuring and patterning potential." The love of materials is especially evident and will amaze anyone unfamiliar with the more experimental side of contemporary designers' imaginations. There is paper pulp, copper wire and human hair alongside more conventional materials, a chandelier knitted from wire flex, a ball gown with 6,500 contraceptive pills in knitted pockets. Conventional product boundaries are crossed in furniture, room screens, shoes and jewelry that challenge definition.

The book also features dozens of clothes, startling and elegant by turn, by the likes of Chalayan, Kenzo, Gaultier and Margiela. As the author points out, knitting fascinates by its versatility and its contrasts. It is a vulnerable and unstable structure compared to weaving, yet its elasticity can give it a special responsiveness to the mobility of the human form. It has an emotional resonance too. Recent experimental treatments are producing previously impossible bonded and other surfaces. Coupled with seamless structures and intentional distortions, contemporary knitwear is experiencing an exciting revival. Thankfully, it seems to be one of knitwear's special and consistent capabilities that, in the hands of adventurous designers, radical or experimental forms do not have to be austere or uncomfortable, they can be sumptuous and sensual. The section on knitwear in performance gives examples of its place in installation and performance art, and an unusual glimpse of ballet and contemporary dance in which the knitwear is a perfect partner to the demands of extreme human movement.

So this book is not the place to look for an account of the new networks of interventionist hand-knitters such as Stitch 'n' Bitch, or to dwell on the demise of old-style domestic knitting. It is unashamedly a celebration of its subject, concentrating on grown-up, high quality design and innovation, at the top end of the fashion market or in the art gallery. Sandy Black has produced a book to inspire knitwear designers and artists too, doubtless practitioners familiar with industrial processes and undaunted by technical issues. There's a long history to the fascination with knit, giving rise to hundreds of illustrated and explanatory books especially since the early nineteenth century, despite the difficulties of making intricate processes comprehensible on the flat page and accessible to newcomers, and she is following in some successful footsteps. This is definitely not a hand-knitter's "how to" book but, in common with her prolific predecessor Miss Lambert in her popular *My Knitting Book* (1844), Sandy Black has arranged her "examples of knitting" so as "to render them comprehensible even to a novice in the art." With her carefully chosen examples, Sandy Black shows how this "art" enthusiastically embraces the better possibilities of the industrial age. Ultimately, by foregrounding innovation and creativity, this is an optimistic book, an antidote to the dull products of globalised textiles and uniform High Streets.

Book Review

Rethinking Decoration: Pleasure and Ideology in the Visual Arts,
David Brett (Cambridge: Cambridge University Press, 2005)

Rethinking Decoration: Pleasure and Ideology in the Visual Arts by David Brett, Emeritus Reader in the History of Design at the University of Ulster offers "theoretical and practical reinterpretation of the decorative by addressing a neglected topic," that is, "the significance of decoration." It is a densely woven text, illustrated with a courageous diversity of images from the local (floor tiles of the Crown Bar, Belfast) to the design iconic (Le Corbusier's Villa La Roche-Jeanneret), to the educative diagrammatic (Kanisza's triangle) to the exoticized historic (the Persian Ardebil Carpet of the sixteenth-century) to the delightfully idiosyncratic (Tudor and Jacobean blackwork embroidery). There is a welcome textual indulgence in Brett's unfolding of his love-labour as he expands and expounds his philosophy of the decorative. Even where periodic and cyclical refusals of decoration are ascendant, Brett finds means by which we can appreciate the verbosity of censure in the articulation of "taste." His exposition of the rhetoric of plainness, restraint, diligence and propriety appeals very much to the spare Puritan section of my soul, while the ornamental oratory, the

aesthetic of the overblown and the saturation of superfluity much critiqued as vulgar excess satisfy the common aspects of my earthy, earthly heart.

There is exceptional scholarship in these chapters, and generous referencing of both key and obscure contributors to the development of design aesthetics, decorative strategies, and concepts of ornament in relation to objects, meanings and spheres of cultural importance. Brett succeeds in his desire to "restore to the decorative some theoretical dignity." Where this restoration segues into the chapter concerned with the "poetics of workmanship," Brett takes us from the theoretical, conceptual, textual into the realm of the dignity of material. Here it is the "fashioning of materials" that grounds all ideas previously examined, locating them in the somatic territory of making with head, heart and hands. Brett urges that the "pleasures to be got from our encounter with the stuff of the world" are those that shape a specifically meaningful poetic of making and materiality. Utility and function are present, but not forefronted, and language is abandoned. Technology is that which marries hand to tool,

REVIEWED BY CATHERINE HARPER

Textile, Volume 4, Issue 1, pp. 130–131
Reprints available directly from the Publishers.
Photocopying permitted by licence only.
© 2006 Berg. Printed in the United Kingdom.

expression is that allowed by each form of making, each type of tool, each set of semantic conventions. The experiential, as explored by Brett via a psychoanalytic identification between material and maternal bodies, is specifically sensual in that it activates touch, taste, smell, sound long before the visual. The body becomes the tool for experience of the decorative, and that decorative is essential, Brett argues, to our human universality. Brett's prose evades romanticism, and the tenderness expressed in his academic writing allows analytic rigour and a fervent intellectualism to keep his reader fixed to the key point. There is a keen eye, a craftsman's eye, steadily at work here.

And for this once-weaver, the subsection titled *Warp and Weft: The Text-tile tectonic* is crucial. Brett has already asserted that there is a shared and transcendent "cross-craft" understanding within material making. So, within the specificity of this text(ile) is the assumption of larger points of communication. Brett uses the modularity and structure of weave patterning apparent in a range of architectures to illuminate how decoration may be achieved, not through the application of ornament, but through the actuality of a manufacturing process which combines the work of a worker, the materiality of a material and the technology of a technique. And he reminds us how a wider range of textile methods—knotting, netting, stitching—continue to interlink sensual pleasure, skilful dexterity, with both cerebral construction of meaning and material construction of things. There is a delightful word-smithing apparent in Brett's playful analysis of the infant's "fingering of materials and her own fingers" in pleasurable experimentation with thread, expanding to the "self-delighting subtlety" of textile hand-making, to the "elaborate abstraction" of the mechanisation of such activity.

Brett's conclusion is that decoration—textile or otherwise— "completes" the buildings, objects and artefacts it affects. Where it is applied with this intent, he argues, it powerfully impacts on civic self-respect as much as on the singular self. This is a potent proclamation for what has been elsewhere dismissed as "mere," "insignificant," "hobbyist," "feminine," and essentially superficial, and I concur with it. Decoration for completion, Brett insists, allows human beings to focus on our achievements, our labours, our value-systems— civic scale activity—while simultaneously attending to the deeply personal and intimate activity of "inviting the eye to dwell and the hand to caress." In both these territories, Brett's thesis determines that decoration, "by completing our world, completes those who live in it—ourselves."

Notes for Contributors

Articles should be approximately 25 pages in length and must include a three-sentence biography of the author(s) and an abstract. Interviews should not exceed 15 pages and do not require an author biography. Exhibition and book reviews are normally 500 to 2,000 words in length. The Publishers will require a disk as well as a hard copy of any contributions (please mark clearly on the disk what word-processing program has been used). Berg accepts most programs with the exception of Clarisworks.

Textile: The Journal of Cloth & Culture will produce one issue a year devoted to a single topic. Persons wishing to organize a topical issue are invited to submit a proposal which contains a hundred-word description of the topic together with a list of potential contributors and paper subjects. Proposals are accepted only after review by the journal editors and in-house editorial staff at Berg.

Manuscripts
Manuscripts should be submitted to one of the editors. Further submission details can be obtained by emailing Janet Gilburt (rooster.gilburt@virgin.net). Manuscripts will be acknowledged by the editor and entered into the review process discussed below. Manuscripts without illustrations will not be returned unless the author provides a self-addressed stamped envelope. Submission of a manuscript to the journal will be taken to imply that it is not being considered elsewhere for publication, and that if accepted for publication, it will not be published elsewhere, in the same form, in any language, without the consent of the editor and publisher. It is a condition of acceptance by the editor of a manuscript for publication that the publishers automatically acquire the copyright of the published article throughout the world. *Textile: The Journal of Cloth & Culture* does not pay authors for their manuscripts nor does it provide retyping, drawing, or mounting of illustrations.

Style
U.S. spelling and mechanicals are to be used. Authors are advised to consult *The Chicago Manual of Style (15th Edition)* as a guideline for style. Webster's Dictionary is our arbiter of spelling. We encourage the use of major subheadings and, where appropriate, second-level subheadings. Manuscripts submitted for consideration as an article must contain: a title page with the full title of the article, the author(s) name and address, a three-sentence biography for each author, and a 200 word abstract. Do not place the author's name on any other page of the manuscript.

Manuscript Preparation
Manuscripts must be typed double-spaced (including quotations, notes, and references cited), one side only, with at least one-inch margins on standard paper using a typeface no smaller than 12pts. The original manuscript and a copy of the text on disk *(please ensure it is clearly marked with the word-processing program that has been used) must* be submitted, along with color *original* photographs (to be returned). Authors should retain a copy for their records. Any necessary artwork must be submitted with the manuscript.

Footnotes
Footnotes appear as "Notes" at the end of articles. Authors are advised to include footnote material in the text whenever possible. Notes are to be numbered consecutively throughout the paper and are to be typed double-spaced at the end of the text. (Do not use any footnoting or end-noting programs that your software may offer as this text becomes irretrievably lost at the typesetting stage.)

References

The list of references should be limited to, and inclusive of, those publications actually cited in the text. References are to be cited in the body of the text in parentheses with the author's last name, the year of original publication, and page number—e.g. (Rouch 1958: 45). Titles and publication information appear as "References" at the end of the article and should be listed alphabetically by author and chronologically for each author. Names of journals and publications should appear in full. Film and video information appears as "Filmography". References cited should be typed double-spaced on a separate page. *References not presented in the style required will be returned to the author for revision.*

Tables

All tabular material should be part of a separately numbered series of "Tables." Each table must be typed on a separate sheet and identified by a short descriptive title. Footnotes for tables appear at the bottom of the table. Marginal notations on manuscripts should indicate approximately where tables are to appear.

Figures

All illustrative material (drawings, maps, diagrams, and photographs) should be designated "Figures." They must be submitted in a form suitable for publication without redrawing. Drawings should be carefully done with black ink on either hard, white, smooth-surfaced board or good quality tracing paper. Ordinarily, computer-generated drawings are not of publishable quality. Color photographs are encouraged by the publishers. Whenever possible, photographs should be 8 × 10 inches. The publishers encourage artwork to be submitted as scanned files (600 dpi or above) on disk or via email. All figures should be clearly numbered on the back and numbered consecutively. All captions should be typed double-spaced on a separate page. Marginal notations on manuscripts should indicate approximately where figures are to appear. While the editors and publishers will use ordinary care in protecting all figures submitted, they cannot assume responsibility for their loss or damage. Authors are discouraged from submitting rare or non-replaceable materials. It is the author's responsibility to secure written copyright clearance on all photographs and drawings that are not in the public domain. Copyright should be obtained for worldwide rights and on-line publishing.

Criteria for Evaluation

Textile: The Journal of Cloth & Culture is a refereed journal. Manuscripts will be accepted only after review by both the editors and anonymous reviewers deemed competent to make professional judgments concerning the quality of the manuscript. Upon request, authors will receive reviewers' evaluations.

Reprints for Authors

Twenty-five reprints of authors' articles will be provided to the first named author free of charge. Additional reprints may be purchased upon request.

Textiles and Text:
Re-establishing the links between archival and object-based research

11, 12 & 13 July 2006

Textile Conservation Centre, University of Southampton, Winchester, UK

This international conference focuses on the interrelationship between archival and bibliographic research and the study of extant objects. Sessions will consider how research can inform our knowledge of textiles and dress, in terms of their production, consumption, dissemination and deterioration and how the study of extant objects can offer unique insights into these contexts. The conference will also examine what tools can be used to investigate textiles produced by cultures that are not predominantly text based and how scientific and photographic analytical techniques can provide clues which cannot readily be gleaned either from objects or written sources.

Papers will cover a wide geographical remit to allow comparison between 'Eastern' and 'Western' cultures and a broad chronological span to encompass issues ranging from pre-history to the present day. A list of speakers and abstracts will appear on our website from the end of February.

For further information, please contact:

The Conference Secretary
The Textile Conservation Centre
Winchester School of Art
University of Southampton
Park Avenue
Winchester SO23 8DL
United Kingdom

Telephone: 02380 597100
Email: contex@soton.ac.uk
website: www.soton.ac.uk/~contex

Third Annual Conference of the Arts & Humanities Research Council
Research Centre for Textile Conservation and Textile Studies

 Arts & Humanities Research Council
 University of Southampton
 MANCHESTER 1824 — The University of Manchester
 UNIVERSITY OF BRADFORD — MAKING KNOWLEDGE WORK

Call for Papers

"Traditions and Trajectories: Education and the Quiltmaker"

A symposium organized by the

INTERNATIONAL QUILT STUDY CENTER, University of Nebraska-Lincoln

March 1-3, 2007

We invite scholars and artists to submit proposals for papers and panel presentations that explore the full breadth of contexts, both formal and informal, in which the quiltmaker's art is learned, studied, applied and handed on. This will include but is not limited to: historical to contemporary, local to global, mainstream to alternative, self-taught to apprentice, church group to cooperative, workshop to academic coursework. We also encourage participants to explore how quiltmakers teach and learn from quilts, how the tactile resonance of quilts influences the education of the women and men who work with them, how changing technology imposes changes in quilt and textile craft education. Though papers relating to the symposium theme will be given preferential consideration, papers concerning any aspect of quilt studies will be considered.

Categories of Presentation:

- Individual papers are expected to be based on original research, are generally illustrated and 20 minutes in length followed by 5 minutes for questions.
- Thematic sessions should include 3 to 4 presenters, and a moderator with a theme based on a particular aspect of education and the quiltmaker or some other theme related to worldwide quiltmaking traditions. Speakers' times are flexible; in general, a total time of one and a half hours is recommended. Panel participants must send a copy of their working paper to their session moderator by December 1, 2006.
- Panel discussions should involve 3 to 4 individuals and a moderator who poses questions to which panelists respond. A total time of one to one and one half hours is recommended for panel discussions.

Symposium Submission Guidelines:

Interested individuals should submit abstracts of 150-200 words with a cover letter and brief resume (maximum 3 pages). Moderators of thematic sessions or panel discussions should submit a proposal of 150-200 words, a cover letter, plus a brief resume (maximum 3 pages) for each participant. Abstracts/proposals should be faxed or postmarked no later than August 15, 2006. (E-mailed submissions will be accepted.)

Submit your abstract/proposal and resume by August 15, 2006, to:

Kathy Moore, 2007 Symposium Coordinator
International Quilt Study Center
University of Nebraska-Lincoln
P.O. Box 830808
Lincoln, NE 68583-0838
iqsc-symposium2@unl.edu
402-472-7232
Fax: 402/472-0640

Symposium Overview:

The International Quilt Study Center's third biennial symposium will feature invited speakers, juried papers, thematic sessions, and panel discussions. The two days of symposium presentations are supplemented by pre-conference tours, including a behind-the-scenes tour of the International Quilt Study Center's state-of-the-art storage facility, curator-led tours of campus exhibitions, and special exhibitions at other venues in the Lincoln area.

Questions or more information contact:
Wendy R. Weiss, 2007 Symposium Co-chair, 402-472-6370
Michael James, 2007 Symposium Co-chair, 402-472-2911
Kathy Moore, 2007 Symposium Coordinator, 402-472-7232
International Quilt Study Center
University of Nebraska-Lincoln
P.O. Box 830808
Lincoln, NE 68583-0838
iqsc-symposium2@unl.edu
Fax: 402/472-0640